THE
EMBROIDERY BOOK

THE EMBROIDERY BOOK

OVER FORTY BEAUTIFULLY SIMPLE PROJECTS FOR YOU AND YOUR HOME

INTRODUCTION BY UNA STUBBS

B. MITCHELL

This edition published in Canada in 1991 by
SMITHBOOKS
113 Merton Street
Toronto, Ontario
M45 1A8

First published in Great Britain in 1989 by Conran Octopus Limited
37 Shelton Street, London WC2H 9HN

ISBN 0 88665 943 4

Typeset by SX Composing Limited
Printed in Hong Kong by

CONTENTS

INTRODUCTION

At last! Here is an embroidery book which caters for all areas of the home and each member of the family, and I'm not talking about babies' bibs and tray cloths. This is a book with totally original ideas: some are exquisitely simple, and others more advanced, yet none is so unusual that in years to come you'll want to fling your effort to the back of the cupboard because it has become dated. I suppose, like any good design – be it for a car, a dress or a piece of furniture – if something has style it never dates. The French have always known that, and what we have here is a stunning collection of French designs.

From the age of 20 I have avidly bought French magazines: it didn't matter a jot that they were only printed in French (of which I speak not one word). I would gaze for hours at the photographs: not just of fashion, but of cooking, interiors and, of course, needlework. I gawped so longingly at Jeanne Moreau's or Brigitte Bardot's luscious houses that I now have a home pretending to be French Provençal in the centre of London! And I copied French clothes by adapting English patterns: for the 60s film *Summer Holiday*, I auditioned wearing my homemade Chanel suit, and clutching an old black bag I had hung with a brassy chain handle.

Then one week there was an article about a lady called Felicia who had embroidered holiday scenes rather than use a camera, and there was a photograph of a wall in her kitchen smothered with enchanting embroidered 'holiday snaps' – it was a feast for the eyes. She has encouraged me in a hobby which is an indisputable joy, and so I must thank Madame Felicia for introducing me to French embroidery so many years ago.

Oh, that I had more hours in the day! I simply don't know which design to copy first from this wonderful collection, they are all so special. I love the Hungarian Duvet Cover and the Dragonfly Bedlinen. I am not as yet a grannie, but I could make the Baby Alphabet coverlet and store it away for later. And how I wish that when I lived in rented accommodation I had known how to cover to advantage the old furniture and ugly fireplaces with lovely embroidery as shown in this book.

I hope my eyesight holds out – I want to go stitching away until the grave! There is so much to choose from here. I can't ever remember looking through an embroidery book that so made me want to get cracking straight away. Many congratulations and thank you to THE EMBROIDERY BOOK for the hours of pleasure you will give to me.

Una Stubbs

8

BASIC ESSENTIALS

The techniques used in this book are all very straightforward, and the patterns easy to use. Most of the designs are shown smaller than actual size: the method used to enlarge them is explained below, as are the standard embroidery techniques and stitches required. Throughout, it is assumed that seams which are not enclosed will be neatened if the fabric is frayable, and that ordinary open seams, described below, will be used unless otherwise stated in the pattern. Skills specific to a particular project are described within the main text.

STARTING OFF

THREADS

Embroidery threads are available in a wide range of weights and colours. The most common threads are cotton or wool, but pure silk, linen, synthetic and metallic threads can also be bought. Some threads are twisted and cannot be divided; while others are made up of several strands which can be separated to give a finer thread. The strands can be put together to give different weight and colour combinations, or thread mixes.

The following threads are used in this book:

Stranded cotton
A lustrous, six-stranded thread which can be separated.

Pearl cotton
A twisted, shiny thread which cannot be divided and is used as a single thread.

Danish flower thread
A soft, fine linen thread.

Tapestry wool
A twisted 4-ply pure wool thread which is hardwearing and mothproofed.

Rug wool
A twisted heavyweight pure wool yarn used for either stitched or tufted rugs.

FABRICS

There are three types of fabrics used for embroidery: plain-weave fabrics, even-weave fabrics and canvas. Plain-weave is the term used to describe any woven fabric, regardless of fibre content. The outline of an embroidery design is usually transferred onto this type of fabric, to act as a guide during the stitching.

Even-weave fabrics, although also plain-weave, have an important difference in the construction of the weave. The warp and weft threads are of identical thickness and the weave of the fabric is perfectly regular. The same number of warp and weft threads occur in a given area, making a regular grid so that stitches can be worked accurately by counting the threads and following a chart. The even-weave fabric group also contains fabrics, usually made of cotton or cotton blends, which have the threads woven together in pairs or in regular blocks.

Canvas is made from stiffened cotton warp and weft threads woven together to produce spaced holes between the threads, giving the fabric a regular grid-like structure. This grid is usually completely covered by the embroidery stitches, often worked from a chart. Canvas is available in different grid sizes (gauges), which indicate the number of threads which can be stitched in a 2.5cm (1in) square. Single canvas has a single-thread grid, and double canvas has pairs of threads forming the grid.

NEEDLES

Crewel, chenille and tapestry needles are the types of needles used for embroidery. They have larger eyes than ordinary sewing needles to accommodate a thicker thread.

Crewel needles
These are medium-length needles used for fine and medium-weight embroidery on plain-weave fabrics.

Chenille needles
Longer and thicker, and with larger eyes than crewel needles, chenille needles are suitable for use with heavier threads and fabrics.

Tapestry needles
Similar in shape to chenille needles, but with a blunt end rather than a sharp point. They are used for embroidery on even-weave fabrics and canvas.

All needles are graded from fine to coarse, with the lower number denoting the coarser needles. Needle sizes are suggested in this book, but you may actually prefer to use a different size according to your personal preference.

EMBROIDERY FRAMES

All embroidery will be more successful if the fabric or canvas is held taut in an embroidery frame. It is not only easier to handle, but the stitches will be more regular and distortion of the fabric is kept to a minimum. There are several types of frame available, and the choice depends on the fabric, the size of the project and your own preference. A simple round frame or hoop is suitable for embroidery on plain-weave fabrics. If the project is quite large, the hoop can be quickly and easily moved along the fabric after a portion of the stitching has been completed. Canvas should be stretched in a rectangular frame, large enough to accommodate the whole piece. The simplest rectangular frame is a wooden stretcher to which the canvas is attached by drawing pins or staples. You can make a stretcher for yourself from four wooden battens joined at the corners, or they are available in a wide range of sizes from art shops. Specialist embroidery frames (slate or rotating frames) are adjustable and stretch the fabric evenly. A hoop or a rectangular frame can be used with even-weave fabric, depending on the size of the project.

ENLARGING A DESIGN

Enlarging the designs in this book to the correct size is not difficult to do successfully, but accurate measuring is important. Basically, the technique consists of dividing the original design into equal squares and then carefully copying the design, square for square, onto a larger grid. First trace the design from the book onto a piece of tracing paper, positioning it centrally, and then follow the diagrams shown on this page. The most accurate way to copy this image is to mark on the larger grid the equivalent points at which the design bisects a line on the smaller grid, and then to join up these marks.

Draw a grid square over the design you have traced, and then draw in a diagonal. Using this line as a guide, mark in the outline of the full-size square or rectangle on a larger piece of tracing paper, and then draw in a grid of the same number of squares, but larger in size, as on the small trace.

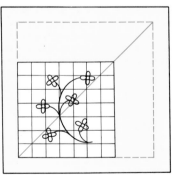

For example, if there is already a grid shown in the book and each square represents a square of 5cm (2in), then draw the large-scale grid to these dimensions. If the design has no grid, but is, say, half size, then draw a squared grid on tracing paper and tape it over the design. Trace the design, and then draw up a large grid, doubling the size and making sure that the top right corner meets a diagonal drawn from the smaller grid.

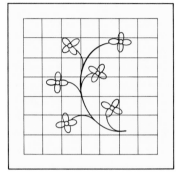

Copy the design square for square onto the larger grid. Once the entire pattern has been transferred, carefully check it back against the original.

TRANSFERRING A DESIGN

When the design has been enlarged to the desired size, you will need to transfer it onto the fabric before beginning the embroidery.

Four transfer methods are described here:

Carbon paper
Position the pattern paper centrally over the right side of the fabric to be embroidered, and pin it to the fabric at each corner. Carefully slide a sheet of dressmakers' carbon paper, carbon side down, between the pattern and the fabric. Draw over the design lines of the pattern with a tracing wheel or a knitting needle used as if it were a pencil.

Transfer pencil
Having drawn the pattern on heavy-duty tracing paper, turn the paper over and trace over the lines with a transfer pencil.

With this traced side facing down onto the fabric, position the pattern paper as required and pin down at each corner. Turn on an iron to a low heat, and press down on the transfer for a few seconds, then lift and move to the next area. Lift up the corner of the paper to make sure that the design is transferring.

Pricking and pouncing
This method is time-consuming but very accurate. Lay the pattern on to a thick wad of fabric – an old blanket would be ideal – and prick holes along the lines of the design using a sharp needle or stiletto. Keep the holes close together to obtain as accurate a copy as possible. Position the design onto the fabric right side up, and pin along the edges to fix the pattern securely. With a felt pad, gently rub pounce (a special-purpose powder available from

craft shops) over the pricked holes. Carefully remove the pattern so as not to smudge the pounce, then join up the dots with a dressmaker's pencil.

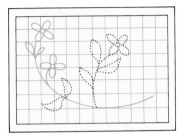

Using a light source
Although accurate, this method will only work with finely-woven fabric of a pale colour. Attach the pattern to a light source such as a window or a light-box, and position the fabric on top. Use a dressmaker's pencil to trace the design.

EMBROIDERY STITCHES

The stitches used for the projects in this book are shown below. Although all are quite simple to work, some – such as satin stitch and long and short stitch – may need a little practice to work them neatly and get good fabric coverage. Follow the diagrams carefully if the stitch is one with which you are unfamiliar.

Work the fabric or canvas in an embroidery hoop or frame as this will help you to keep the stitches regular. Remember not to pull the threads too tightly, since this can distort the shape. The individual instructions will give you details of how to work the designs, where to start stitching, how many strands of thread to use, and suggested needle sizes.

Do not use a knot on the back of the fabric or canvas as an unsightly bulge will appear on the right side. Instead, leave a short length of the thread hanging, use the needleful of thread and then carefully secure both the ends on the wrong side by threading them through the stitches.

Before beginning a project, it is a good idea to practise sewing stitches with which you are unfamiliar on a spare piece of canvas or fabric. You may also wish to experiment with different colours and combinations of threads, and even with alternative stitches. In this way, you can either subtly or radically alter the design to suit your particular taste and requirements.

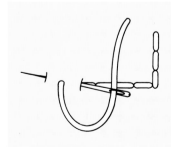

straight stitch

hemming stitch

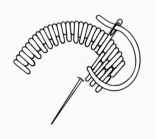

darning stitch

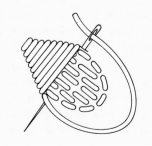

satin stitch

feather stitch

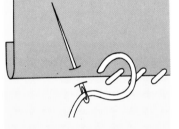

cross stitch

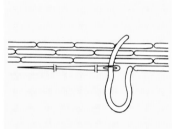

buttonhole stitch

encroaching satin stitch

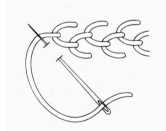

back stitch

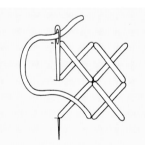

chain stitch

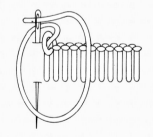

long and short stitch

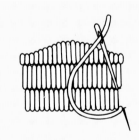

padded satin stitch

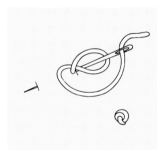

Chinese knots

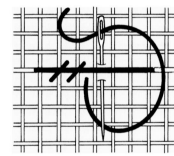

tent stitch

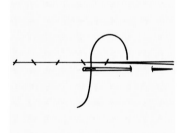

trammed half cross stitch

NOTE: Some of the stitches used in this book have been shown with specific projects: **antique hem stitch** (drawn-thread) see page 108, **closed herringbone stitch** see page 158, **French knots** see page 184.

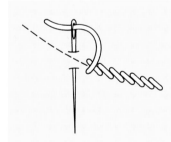

stem stitch

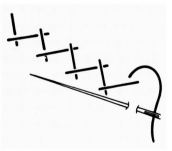

couching

slip stitch

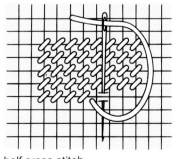

half cross stitch

seed stitch

herringbone stitch

FINISHING OFF

PRESSING

Embroidery on fabric will need a light pressing to smooth out any wrinkles in the fabric caused by the stitching.

Before pressing, pad the ironing board with a thick, folded towel and lay the embroidery over it face down.

Cover the embroidery with a damp piece of thin cotton fabric and press lightly, letting the iron just touch the pressing cloth. Take care not to crush heavily stitched areas. Let the embroidery dry thoroughly.

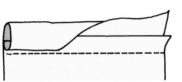

SEAMS

Plain seam
Place the two fabric pieces with right sides together, raw edges level; pin and stitch together 1.5cm (⅝in) from the raw edges. Work a few stitches in reverse at each end of the seam to secure the threads.

The simplest method of neatening the seam allowance edges is by zigzag stitching on a sewing-machine. Use a short, narrow stitch worked slightly in from the raw edge. If the fabric has a tendency to fray, use a larger stitch and work over the raw edge. Where the fabric is fine, turn under the raw edge and either zigzag stitch or straight stitch. If neatening by hand, oversew the raw edges: work from left to right, taking the thread diagonally over the edge and keeping the stitches about

3mm (⅛in) apart. If the fabric tends to fray, work a row of straight stitching first, then oversew over the edge. If the fabric is very heavy, simply pink the edges using a pair of pinking shears.

Flat fell seam
This is a self-neatening seam that is very strong and distinctive. Place the two fabric pieces with right sides together 1.5cm (⅝in) from the raw edges. Press the seam allowance to one side. Trim down the lower seam allowance to 6mm (¼in). Fold the upper seam allowance over, enclosing the lower seam allowance. Press the folded allowance flat against the fabric; pin and stitch close to the folded edge.

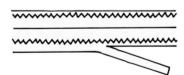

French seam
This is a self-finishing seam. Place the two fabric pieces with wrong sides together; pin and stitch 6mm (¼in) from the raw edges. Press the seam open. Refold with right sides together; pin and stitch 1cm (⅜in) from the seamed edge.

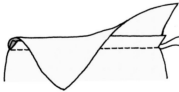

FASTENINGS

How to insert a zip
Pin and tack the seam into which the zip is to be inserted. Stitch in from each, or from one, end of the seam, leaving an

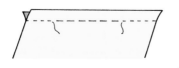

opening the same length as the zip. Press the tacked seam open. Place the zip face down over the seam allowances with the bottom stop 3mm (⅛in) beyond the tacking at one side and with the teeth centred over the tacked seam. Tack in place through all layers 6mm (¼in) on either side of the teeth. Turn to the right side. Stitch the zip in place using a zipper foot on the sewing-machine or backstitch by hand, following the tacking lines at the sides and pivoting the stitching at the bottom corners or at both ends.

BIAS STRIPS

To cut the fabric on the bias, fold the fabric so that the selvedge (warp threads) lies exactly parallel to the weft threads. The fold formed is the true cross. Cut along the fold and then cut bias strips parallel to this edge.

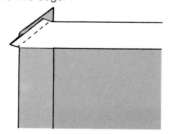

Mark off the strips using pins or a marking pen and cut out. To join strips together, place two strips with right sides together on the straight of the grain, as shown, and stitch together taking 6mm (¼in) seams. Trim off points level with the side edges and press seams open.

MITRING THE CORNERS

This method of finishing corners will ensure a neat, crisp finish.

Mitring fabric
Fold over a narrow hem along each edge of the fabric and press. Trim the corner to reduce

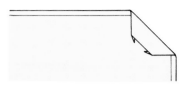

bulk, then turn the corner over and press. Fold over the two sides as shown, and pin in place. Hand or machine stitch along the hem. Hand stitch the diagonal join if the hem is quite wide.

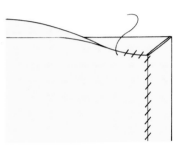

Mitring canvas
Always block the canvas (see below) before finishing the edges. Trim the corner of the surplus canvas to reduce the bulk. Turn the canvas over to the corner of the embroidery.

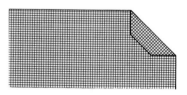

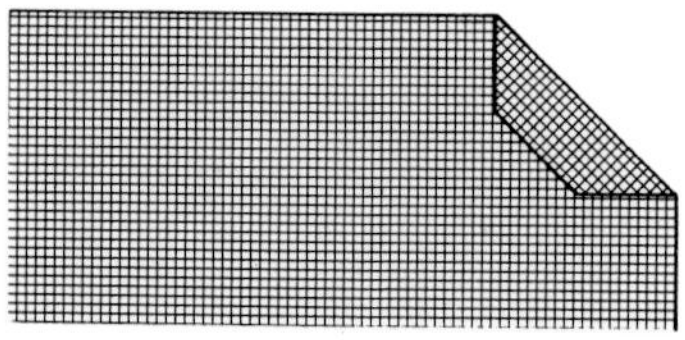

Fold in the side edges, making sure that the corner is square, and tack in place. Then secure the edge and the mitred corner with a row of hand stitching.

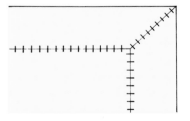

Mitring a fabric band
Fold the fabric band in half lengthways, raw edges together. Fold up the raw edges

in line with the folded edge and press. Cut along the fold lines. Repeat at the opposite end of the strip, but so that the diagonal edge is facing in the opposite direction. Repeat with all strips. Unfold two adjoining strips and place with right sides together and pointed ends matching. Pin and stitch the end, beginning and ending the

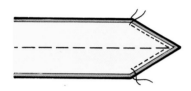

stitching 1.5cm (⅝in) from either end of the seam. Trim and turn to the right side, refolding the strip in half. Repeat, to form each mitred corner. Place one edge to the main piece of fabric with right sides together; pin and stitch. Turn under remaining edge of band and slipstitch over previous stitches on the wrong side.

Mitring binding

Unfold one edge of binding and place against the raw fabric edge. Pin and stitch in place along the first side up to the seam allowance at the turning point. Press up the binding over the stitched side at a 45 degree angle. Stitch the next side beginning at the turning point. Trim and turn the binding over the raw edge to the wrong side folding the excess binding on both sides into mitres. Slipstitch

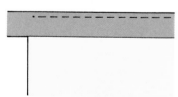

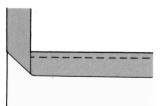

the remaining folded edge of binding over previous stitches on the wrong side. If the binding is wide, stitch across the corner on the right side of the fabric before turning the binding over the raw edge. Trim and press open. Pleat the excess fabric into a mitre on the wrong side.

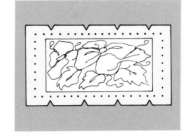

BLOCKING

Canvaswork should be blocked to straighten the grain of the canvas, which becomes distorted during the stitching, even when an embroidery frame has been used. For blocking, you will need: a piece of wood or blockboard larger than the embroidery and covered with a sheet of clean polythene; rustproof tacks; a hammer; a steel rule or tape measure; a water spray or sponge.

If the canvas has a selvedge, cut small nicks along it to ensure that it stretches evenly. Damp the canvaswork with the spray or a wet sponge and place it face down on the board.

Lightly hammer tacks in the middle of the top and bottom of the surplus canvas, stretching the canvas gently downwards. Repeat for each side, checking that the warp and weft threads of the canvas are at right angles to each other.

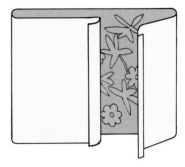

Working outwards from the centre of each side, insert more tacks at 2cm (¾in) intervals, stretching the canvas gently as you proceed. When you have done all four sides, check the size and shape of the canvas to make sure the stretching is even and adjust the tacks where necessary. Hammer all the tacks in securely. Spray or sponge the canvas so that it is evenly damp, and leave it to dry at room temperature for several days. A second blocking may be needed to straighten strongly vertical or horizontal designs.

CUSHION COVER

This cushion cover is made quite simply from one folded piece of fabric, and does not require a zip or fasteners. For a snug fit, the cushion pad should measure about 2.5cm (1in) more in each direction than one side

of the sewn cover.

Neaten the short edges of the fabric by turning a narrow hem and machine stitching.

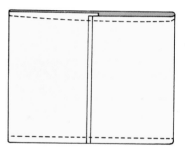

Fold the fabric as shown, with the right side facing in, making sure that the wider flap will be on top when you turn the cover

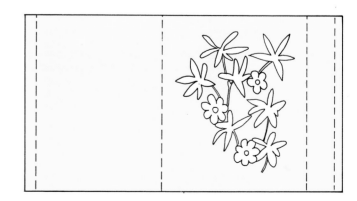

right side out. Pin the sides.

Machine stitch along either side of the cushion cover, stitching across the overlapping fabric folds which will form a flap.

Turn the cushion cover right side out, gently pushing the corners out fully. Press well.

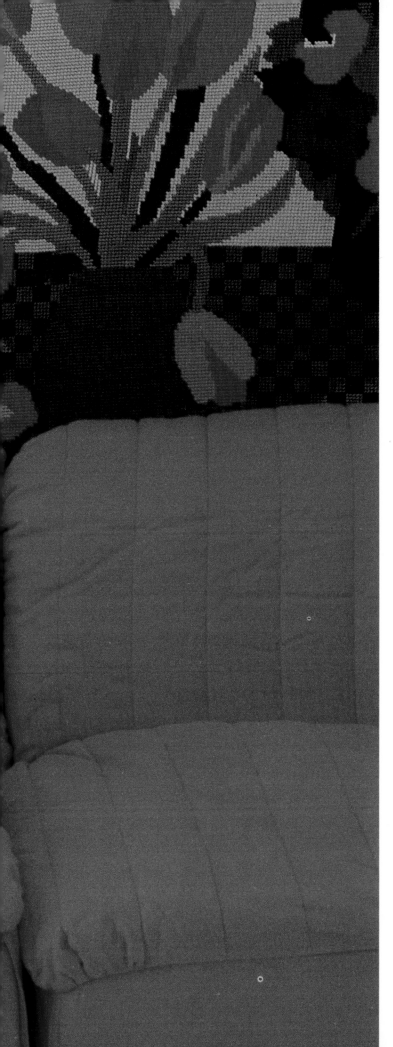

CANVASWORK

CRAZY CROSS STITCH

A far cry from the conventional flower-patterned needlepoint, this unusual cross-stitch design features a bold, humorous medley of letters, symbols and colours, with elements of both 1930s and 1950s decorative styles. The result is a colourful rug that will harmonize with most modern settings. If you want to add a personal touch, you could easily substitute your initials for some of the letters, keeping to the same large block capitals with drawing pin circles at the joins.

Size Approximately 159cm × 138cm (63½in × 55in).

MATERIALS

1.8m × 1.6m (2yd × 1¾yd) of 4-gauge rug canvas	Large tapestry or rug needle
Strong sewing thread	Fine-tip waterproof felt marker
	Wide masking tape

Threads
Pingouin rug yarn (if this is not available, substitute the same colours from another range): 16 balls of **grey** 30; nine balls of **black** 36; four balls each of **red** 43, **yellow** 61 and **orange** 52; three balls each of **bright** **blue** 60, **pink** 51 and **white** 05; two balls each of **turquoise** 55, **sky blue** 65, **jade green** 71, **green** 58 and **rose pink** 15; one ball each of **brown** 08, **French blue** 34 and **brick** 14

Embroidery stitches
Cross stitch worked in two journeys (see below); each square on the chart represents one cross stitch.
Herringbone stitch for finishing the edges.

METHOD

▦ Draw a vertical line with the waterproof marker down the centre of the canvas, taking care not to cross any vertical threads. Mark the central horizontal line in the same way. Rule corresponding lines across the chart to find the centre of the design.
▦ Bind the edges of the canvas with masking tape to prevent the threads unravelling. Begin stitching at the centre of the canvas, working outwards from the centre of the design and following the chart square by square. To make the canvas easier to handle, roll up those areas on which you are not working.
▦ Make each horizontal line of cross stitch in two journeys. Stitch the left to right diagonals on the first journey and complete the crosses on the second journey by filling in the right to left diagonals.
▦ When all the stitching has been completed, block the embroidery (see page 15) if it has pulled out of shape. Trim the surplus canvas away leaving a margin of 10cm (4in) of unworked canvas all around the embroidery.
▦ On the reverse of the rug, turn in the margin (see page 14 for instructions on mitring corners) and secure the edges with a row of herringbone stitch in strong thread.
▦ Alternatively, use strips of carpet webbing, overlapping them at the corners. Backstitch the strips to the rug, then mitre and stitch them as shown.

KEY

30 □ 1
37 ⊠ 2
43 ⊡ 3
52 ◣ 4
61 □ 5
51 ◩ 6
15 □ 7
60 □ 8
14 ⊞ 9
05 ⊟ 10
55 ■ 11
65 ◹ 12
71 □ 13
58 ◿ 14
08 ⊙ 15
34 □ 16

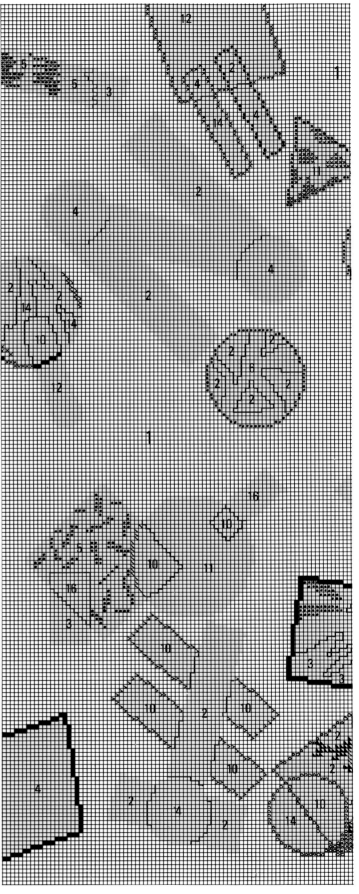

COUNTRYSIDE MOSAIC

Each of the nine canvas squares that make up this tapestry mosaic contains a different wildlife scene, but they cleverly combine to create a complete picture – poppies and ladybirds, frogs on lily pads, butterflies and milkweed, snails and dandelions are just some of them. If you feel that the complete mosaic is beyond you, make up just a couple of the individual scenes.

MATERIALS

9 squares of single thread 12-gauge canvas, each 36cm (14½in) × 36cm (14½in)
Tapestry needle size 18 or 20
90cm (3ft) × 90cm (3ft) beige

cotton fabric
Matching sewing thread
Fine-tip waterproof felt marker
Embroidery frame

Threads
DMC tapestry wool in the colours given beside each panel.

Embroidery Stitches
Tent stitch, Chinese knots, straight stitch, herringbone stitch, back stitch.

Each square of the design is complete in itself, but can be combined with others to make a larger scene. When all the squares are embroidered and blocked, arrange them as shown in the diagrams opposite. Join the squares with flat seams using back stitch (see page 12), and press open.

For a larger bedspread, slipstitch the completed embroidery on to a plain bedspread. Move the panel around the bedspread until the desired effect is achieved. For a wall hanging, make a casing at the top and bottom edges and insert two bamboo canes and hang with a cord.

METHOD

▦ Draw a vertical line with the marker through the centre of each canvas square, taking care not to cross any vertical threads. Mark the central horizontal line in the same way. Then rule corresponding lines across the chart to find the centre of the design.

▦ Work each of the individual canvas squares in an embroidery frame.

▦ Work the designs outwards from the centre in tent stitch and pick out the details in Chinese knots and straight stitch as shown in the photographs.

▦ When all the squares have been embroidered, block each one carefully (see page 15), making sure that they are all the same size: each blocked square should measure approximately 25cm (10in) × 25cm (10in).

▦ Following the diagram, join the squares into three strips of three squares, by making a flat back-stitched seam between each square. Press each seam open.

▦ Join the strips together in the same way, and again press each seam open.

▦ On the reverse of the cover, turn in the surplus canvas round the edge (see page 14 for instructions on mitring corners) and secure it with a row of herringbone stitch.

▦ To make the lining, cut an 82cm (33in) square from the beige fabric. Turn and press a hem round the edge to make a 78cm (31in) square. Slipstitch the lining to the bedcover and press it gently, taking care not to crush the stitches.

1

1. Dandelions and snail
green 7320, 7347, 7370, 7548;
brown 7419, 7468, 7526;
turquoise 7302; *orange* 7767;
beige 7465; *cream* 7141; *blue*

7800; *grey* 7331, 7620; *yellow*
7473, 7727, 7742, 7905; *white*

2. Bee with flowers
cream 7503; *pink* 7135, 7136,

7640; *grey* 7618, 7624; *blue*
7799; *green* 7339, 7363, 7396,
7398; *turquoise* 7592; *brown*
7417, 7419, 7479, 7485, 7713,
7999; *black*; *white*

3. Ladybird and poppies
green 7347, 7427, 7770; *tan*
7947; *red* 7107, 7606; *blue*
7799; *brown* 7401, 7415, 7419,
7801; *grey* 7618, 7713; *yellow*

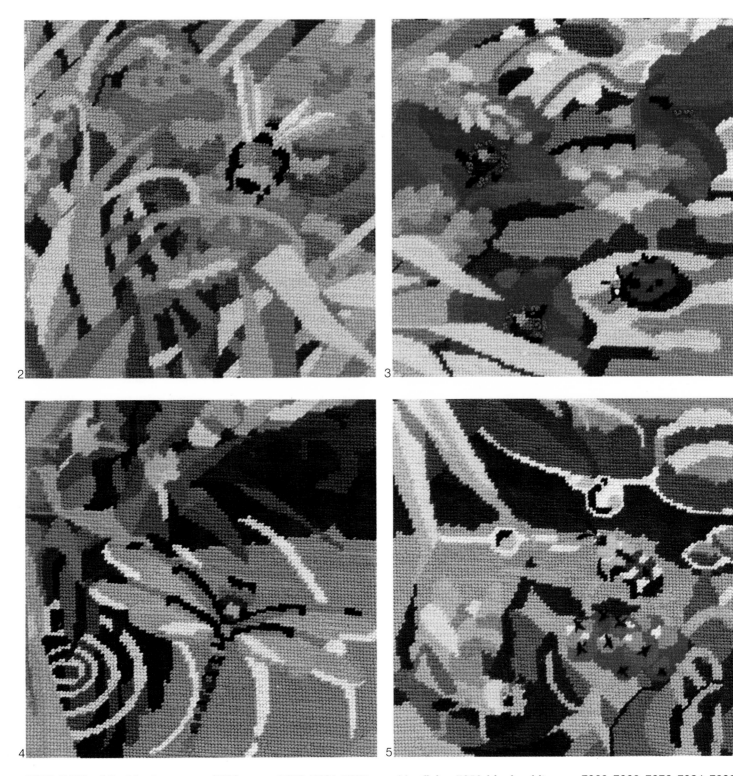

7078, 7485; **white**; **black**; **ecru**

4. Dragonfly and flowers
yellow 7484, 7504, 7579, 7678, 7843; **brown** 7417, 7469, 7479,

7526; **green** 7353, 7362, 7363, 7389, 7404, 7408, 7427, 7429; **blue** 7243, 7791; **turquoise** 7302, 7326, 7329, 7592, 7690; **mauve** 7245; **cream** 7493;

kingfisher 7650; **black**; **white**

5. Grasshopper and berries
brown 7513, 7526, 7548, 7713, 7833, 7999; **green** 7346, 7353,

7362, 7363, 7376, 7384, 7392, 7396, 7493, 7861; **yellow** 7473, 7485, 7785; **beige** 7450; **red** 7606, 7666, 7946; **turquoise** 7302, 7592; **black**; **white**

6

7

8

9

6. Frog and waterlily
brown *7249, 7355, 7490, 7801;*
green *7362, 7636, 7384, 7540;*
yellow *7485, 7677, 7678;* **pink**
7356, 7543, 7950; **black**; **white**

7. Newt and flowers
green *7320, 7362, 7363, 7384,*

7389, 7393, 7398, 7890; **brown**
7249, 7512, 7526, 7999; **yellow**
7678, 7782, 7784, 7785; **cream**
7501; **beige** *7450;* **turquoise**
7592; **black**; **white**

8. Butterflies and flowers
brown *7514, 7538, 7713, 7780;*

green *7320, 7363, 7384, 7387,*
7583, 7890; **yellow** *7504, 7678,*
7786; **pink** *7255;* **mauve** *7245;*
turquoise *7996;* **orange** *7505,*
7946; **red** *7666;* **blue** *7317,*
7796; **tan** *7457;* **black**; **white**;
ecru

9. Beetles and flowers
yellow *7677, 7784, 7786;* **green**
7320, 7367, 7386, 7389, 7424,
7548, 7583, 7890, 7956; **brown**
7479, 7526, 7713, 7845, 7846;
beige *7450, 7463;* **mauve** *7245;*
pink *7255;* **blue** *7317, 7820,*
7995; **white**; **ecru**

FRESH FLOWERS

Transform an old chair by stitching a new needle-point cover, decorated with a colourful bouquet of flowers, and turn an eyesore into an elegant conversation piece: the idea is scarcely new, but the reason for its perennial success is that it works so well and so beautifully. The background in this case is given interest by a simple geometric design and in order to vary the effect the French artist used a larger scale of canvas for the seat than for the back and sides of the chair, changing the size of the pattern.

Size Adjustable to fit any chair; the flower bouquet measures approximately 25cm (10in) from top to bottom and 20cm (8in) across.

MATERIALS

Single-thread 16-gauge canvas for the back and side panels	wooden stretchers large enough to accommodate each piece of canvas
Single-thread 14-gauge canvas for the seat cushion	Fine-tip waterproof felt marker
Tapestry needles size 20 and 18	Medium-tip felt marker
Rotating embroidery frame or	

Note Chairs differ greatly in shape and design, and unless you have advanced upholstery skills you will probably choose to have your chair reupholstered professionally, so we have not explained how to fit the cover. Take all measurements very carefully (if possible, remove the old upholstery and measure this flat), making generous allowance for tuck-ins and seam allowances.

Threads

For the bouquet, DMC tapestry wools: one skein each of **red** 7107, 7606 and 7946, **orange** 7439, **mauve** 7120, **violet** 7243, 7251, 7255 and 7709, **peach** 7917, **pink** 7133, 7204, 7260, 7600, 7603 and 7804, **blue** 7304, 7313, 7314, 7317 and 7800, **green** 7327, 7369, 7384, 7386 7420, 7424, 7549, 7583, 7771, 7912 and 7956, **yellow** 7433, 7681 and 7725, **beige** 7423 and 7579, **cream** 7745, **ecru** and **white**

For the back, side panels, cushion cover and bouquet background the following colours of DMC tapestry wool are used:
green 7369, 7386, 7420 and 7424.

Embroidery stitches

Half cross stitch, slanting satin stitch and straight stitch.

Note
To calculate the amount of thread needed for your chair, embroider a 10cm (4in) square of the pattern to use as a guide, stitching as follows: main colour 7424, second colour 7369, third colour 7386 and fourth colour 7420.

METHOD

▦ Measure each section of the chair widthwise and lengthwise. Draw the outline of each section on the appropriate canvas, bearing in mind that the finished pieces of embroidery should be approximately 1cm (⅜in) larger than these measurements to allow for turnings. Allow at least 10cm (4in) of surplus canvas round each piece for mounting in the embroidery frame, for blocking, and for the upholstery.
▦ Trace the bouquet design for the back of the chair and then enlarge it to the required dimensions (see page 10). Strengthen the design lines with the medium felt marker.
▦ Place the canvas for the back panel over the design, centring the bouquet inside the drawn outline. The design lines will now be visible

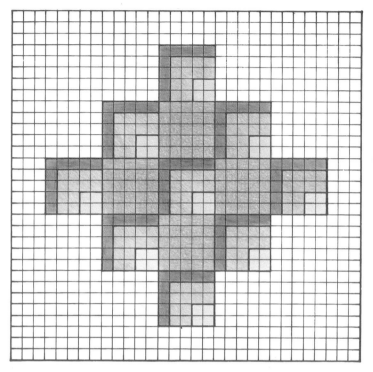

through the canvas. Using the waterproof felt marker, trace the design carefully onto the canvas.

▦ Mount the canvas in the embroidery frame or a stretcher and begin the embroidery by working the flowers in irregular straight stitch. Work with the tapestry wool divided in half in the smaller needle and use the photograph as a colour blending and stitch guide. When all the flowers have been completed, fill in the background between them in half cross stitch, using the green thread 7424.

▦ Work the geometric pattern round the central motif in slanting satin stitch and half cross stitch. Follow the chart carefully and again work with the tapestry wool divided in half.

▦ Work the geometric pattern on the two side panels in the same way.

▦ Embroider the geometric pattern for the cushion sections on the coarser canvas, using the tapestry wool undivided in the larger needle.

▦ When all the embroidery has been completed block the sections (see page 15) if they have pulled out of shape, paying special attention to the geometric pattern, which should be perfectly regular.

KEY

1	*7107*
2	*7439*
3	*7606*
4	*7946*
5	*7600*
6	*7603*
7	*7804*
8	*7133*
9	*7204*
10	*7260*
11	*7255*
12	*7709*
13	*7251*
14	*7120*
15	*7243*
16	*7917*
17	*7433*
18	*7725*
19	*7681*
20	*7745*
21	*7579*
22	*7423*
23	*ecru*
24	*white*
25	*7369*
26	*7384*
27	*7386*
28	*7420*
29	*7424*
30	*7549*
31	*7583*
32	*7771*
33	*7327*
34	*7912*
35	*7956*
36	*7304*
37	*7313*
38	*7314*
39	*7317*
40	*7800*

Enlarge 1½ times

FRUIT NEEDLEPOINT

The soft colours of this needlepoint fruit basket suggest the ageing tones of gentle Dutch seventeenth-century still lifes. The embroidery is worked in half cross stitch on linen – the natural colour of the fabric provides the perfect neutral background for the fine needlework.

MATERIALS

60cm (24in) × 80cm (32in) light brown even-weave 24-gauge linen

Crewel needle size 5 or 6
Embroidery hoop

Threads

Danish flower threads –
1 skein of each of the following colours: **green** *40, 222, 223, 302;* **red** *53, 93;* **violet** *5, 230;* **yellow** *28, 225;* **fawn** *7*
DMC stranded cotton –
3 skeins of **green** *989*
2 skeins of each of the following colours:
green *472, 3346, 3348;* **coral** *353;* **peach** *754;* **beige** *644*
1 skein of each of the following colours:
green *368, 471, 581, 3051, 3052, 3053, 3347;* **bronze** *733, 734;* **rust** *355, 356;* **tan** *922;* **coral** *352;* **peach** *758, 945, 950, 951;* **pink** *316, 760, 778, 948;* **mauve** *3041, 3042;* **yellow** *745, 3078;* **cream** *746;* **gold** *437, 677, 833, 834, 3046;* **fawn** *422, 738;* **brown** *420, 640, 642;* **beige** *437, 712, 739;* **grey** *452, 453, 646, 647, 3023*

Embroidery Stitch

Half cross stitch: each square on the chart represents one half cross stitch worked over two vertical and two horizontal fabric threads.

METHOD

▦ Run a vertical and a horizontal line of tacking through the centre of the linen to correspond with the centre lines on the chart.
▦ Work with the fabric stretched in an embroidery hoop, moving the hoop as necessary.
▦ Embroider the design outwards from the centre in half cross stitch, following the picture on page 33 and using the colours and threads indicated: the main part of the picture is worked using five strands of the stranded cotton, while some areas are stitched with a combination of Danish flower thread and stranded cotton threaded

through the needle together.
▦ When the embroidery is completed, place it face down on a well-padded surface and press lightly, taking care not to crush the stitches.
▦ If the fabric has become distorted during the stitching, it will need to be blocked (see page 15). The embroidery should be framed professionally.

A.   Vine leaves, tendrils and stalks
green 40, 47, 223, 368, 471, 472, 581, 989, 3051, 3052, 3053, 3446, 3347, 3348
brown 420, 640
grey 646, 647
fawn 422

B.   Basket
grey 646, 3023
rust 356
beige 644
fawn 7
green 222, 302, 3052

C.   Cherries
pink 948
peach 754, 758
rust 355, 356
coral 352
tan 922
red 53, 93
green 368

D. Green grapes
bronze 734
green 472
cream 746
fawn 422, 738
gold 833, 834, 3046, 3047
yellow 225, 3078

E.   Black grapes
mauve 3041, 3042
violet 5, 230
pink 316, 778
green 581

F.   Apple
pink 760, 948
peach 754, 950
green 472
coral 353
beige 350, 712
yellow 745, 3078

G.   Left pear
peach 945, 950, 951
beige 437, 739
gold 677
green 223, 368, 3348
yellow 28
pink 948
fawn 422

H.   Right pear
peach 945, 950
beige 437, 712
gold 677
green 472
yellow 3078
fawn 422
brown 642
grey 452, 647

I.   Peach at the back
peach 754
pink 760, 948
coral 353
yellow 745
beige 712
fawn 738
grey 452, 453

J.   Front peach
peach 754, 950
pink 760
coral 352, 353
yellow 745, 3078
beige 712
grey 452, 453, 647

K.   Fruit inside basket
green 472, 989, 3051, 3346, 3347
rust 355

The diagram indicates the different fruits and can be used with this list of colours.

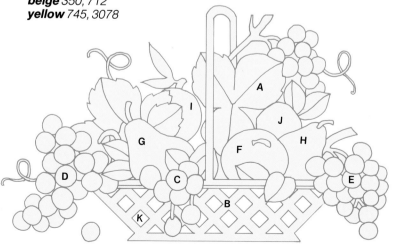

TULIP TIME

Use it as a wall hanging, an unusual table runner or even as a mat: whichever you choose, this bright needlepoint picture with its vivid, life-size tulips and anemones will catch the eye and lift the spirits. The zingy reds and pinks, glowing all the more against the green contrast of the leaves, blend happily with the clean, simple lines of modern furnishings.

Size Approximately 200cm × 60cm (80in × 24in).

MATERIALS

2.2m × 70cm (2½yd × 28in) of double-thread 12-gauge canvas
2.2m (2½yd) of 90cm (36in)-wide cotton fabric in a neutral colour, for the lining
Matching strong sewing thread
Tapestry needle size 18 or 20
Fine-tip waterproof felt marker

Medium-tip black felt marker
Rotating embroidery frame, large enough to accommodate the width of the canvas
Wide masking tape
205cm (82in) strip of 10cm (4in) wide webbing, optional, for a casing if the panel is to be hung

Threads
DMC tapestry yarn: one skein each of green 7342, 7370, 7604 and 7912, pink 7153, yellow 7784 and 7973, and mauve 7247; two skeins each of blue 7797, green 7345, 7386 and 7540, ecru, pink 7103, 7106, 7135 and 7151, red 7137, yellow 7726, and mauve 7245; three skeins each of green 7596 and

7988, pink 7136, and mauve 7243; four skeins of green 7344; five skeins each of red 7640; six skeins each of black, and green 7861; seven skeins each of red 7606 and 7666; eight skeins of pink 7157; nine skeins each of green 7943 and 7547, and pink 7155; 17 skeins each of blue 7820 and 7995, and 29 skeins of beige 7280

Embroidery stitches
Trammed half cross stitch for the plain background, flowers and pots; half cross stitch for the chequerboard background, and herringbone stitch for finishing the edges.

34

METHOD

THE EMBROIDERY

▦ Trace the design and then enlarge it to the dimensions given. Strengthen the design lines with the felt marker.

▦ Place the canvas over the design, leaving a 10cm (4in) margin of surplus canvas around all the edges. The design lines will now be visible through the canvas. Using the waterproof felt marker, trace the design carefully onto the canvas.

▦ Bind the two long edges of the canvas with masking tape to prevent them fraying and then mount the canvas in the rotating embroidery frame.

▦ Starting at one edge and working each area of colour separately, embroider the chequerboard background in half cross stitch and the rest of the design in trammed half cross stitch.

▦ When all the embroidery has been completed, remove the embroidery frame.

▦ Block the embroidery (see page 15) if it has pulled out of shape, paying special attention to the chequerboard pattern, in which the squares should be regular.

FINISHING THE PANEL

▦ Leaving a margin of 5cm (2in) all around the embroidered area, trim away the surplus canvas.

Mitring the corners, turn the unworked edges to the back and secure them with herringbone stitch.

To make the lining, cut a rectangle of lining fabric 2.5cm (1in) larger than the finished embroidery on all edges. Turn in and press a generous 2.5cm (1in) single hem all around, making sure

that the finished size of the lining is slightly smaller than the embroidery.

If you wish to hang the picture, turn in the short ends of the webbing by 2.5cm (1in). Position the webbing 2cm (¾in) below the top edge of the lining and machine along the top edge. Lay the lining on a flat surface; take the hanging

pole and fold the webbing over it. Pin along the bottom edge of the webbing; remove the pole, and then stitch along the pinned edge.

Fold the lining vertically in half, bringing right sides together. Using locking stitch, in which the thread is taken alternately through the back of the embroidery and then through the lining, join the

lining to the back of the finished embroidery down the centre. Working first out to one side then out to the other, join the lining to the back of the embroidery with vertical lines of stitching approximately 25cm (10in) apart, always taking care not to stitch through the webbing sleeve. Finish by slipstitching around all edges.

KEY

a 7342	**j** 7345	**t** 7245	**D** 7606
b 7370	**k** 7386	**u** 7596	**E** 7666
c 7604	**l** 7540	**v** 7988	**F** 7157
d 7912	**m** ecru	**w** 7136	**G** 7943
e 7153	**n** 7103	**x** 7243	**H** 7155
f 7784	**o** 7106	**y** 7344	**I** 7820
g 7973	**p** 7135	**z** 7547	**J** 7995
h 7247	**q** 7151	**A** 7640	
i 7797	**r** 7137	**B** black	
	s 7726	**C** 7861	

PANSY BAG

Pansies – *pensées* means thoughts – are just the motif for a useful carry-all for books, holiday things, or weekend bits and pieces. The bag is stitched in sturdy cotton first and the embroidered canvas panel is attached afterwards.

MATERIALS

80cm (32in) × 115cm (45in) heavy grey cotton fabric
19cm (7½in) × 46cm (18½in) grey lining fabric
50cm (20in) × 55cm (22in) double-thread 10-gauge canvas

16cm (6½in) × 43cm (17in) stout card
Grey sewing thread
Fine-tip waterproof pen
Fabric glue
Tapestry needle size 18 or 20
Embroidery frame

Threads
Anchor tapestry wool
TARTAN BACKGROUND
4 skeins of **grey** 400; 3 skeins of **beige** 438; 5 skeins of **blue** 147; 5 skeins of **green** 164; 2 skeins of **green** 506.
THE PANSIES
1 skein of each colour:
green 213, 215, 243, 265, 861; **yellow** 264, 288, 290, 297, 305, 306, 729; **beige** 377, 390, 711, 732; **white** 402; **pink** 337, 421, 570, 661, 732, 835, 892; **blue** 850, 851

Embroidery Stitch
Half cross stitch: each square on the chart represents one half cross stitch.

METHOD

THE PANSY EMBROIDERY:

▦ Draw a 43cm (17in) × 36cm (14½in) rectangle centrally on the canvas with the felt marker. Then draw a vertical and a horizontal line in the centre of this rectangle, taking care not to cross any threads running the opposite way. Rule corresponding lines across the printed chart to find the centre.

▦ Work with the canvas in a frame. Begin stitching at the centre of the canvas, working outwards and following the chart square by square. Embroider the pansy design first and then fill in the background with the tartan pattern.

▦ Block the finished piece of embroidery (see page 15).

▦ Trim the surplus canvas away leaving a margin of 2.5cm (1in) all round the embroidery. Turn in the margin (see page 14 for instructions on mitring corners) and tack round the edge.

TO MAKE THE BAG:

▦ Cut out the fabric as shown in the cutting layout. Join the front and back pieces together along the shortest sides using a run and fell seam with a seam allowance of 1.5cm (⅝in). Turn over 1cm (⅜in) followed by 2.5cm (1in) along the top of the bag, right-side up, to make a double hem; topstitch 5mm (¼in) away from the edge.

▦ Fold each strap piece in half lengthways with the right side of the fabric on the inside. Stitch 1cm (⅜in) from the edge. Turn the straps to the right side and press flat. Top stitch all the way round 5mm (¼in) from the edge.

▦ Pin one strap to the front of the bag and one to the back along the lines indicated on the pattern and stitch in place securely.

▦ Turn the bag inside out and pin the base piece in place (with a seam allowance of 1.5cm (⅝in)). Stitch round the base twice. Turn the bag right side out and slipstitch the embroidered panel to the front.

▦ Cover the card with the lining fabric, as shown in the diagram, and let the glue dry thoroughly, then drop the base into the bag and push well down.

Assemble the bag by joining the front and back sections. Make the straps and attach them securely before sewing the base in position. Slipstitch the canvaswork panel to the front of the bag before inserting the stiffened base panel

Cutting layout:

strap cut 2

bottom cut 1

back and front cut 2

1 sq. = 10 cm.

Tartan pattern		10	265	7	337	3	661
1	400	11	288	8	570	4	402
2	506			9	243	5	732
3	438	**Flowers B**				6	421
4	147	1	661	**Flowers D**		7	892
		2	570	1	850	8	570
Flowers A		3	421	2	306	9	711
1	850	4	305	3	305	10	297
2	264			4	297	11	243
3	306	**Flowers C**		5	402		
4	711	1	851	6	732	**Leaves F**	
5	390	2	290	7	570	1	213
6	243	3	402			2	215
7	297	4	390	**Flowers E**		3	861
8	402	5	835	1	850	4	438
9	305	6	729	2	306	5	377

COUNTRY CONTENTMENT

Sit down to a refreshing cup of tea, secure in the knowledge that there is another cup in the pot, kept warm by a teacosy like a romantic rural idyll: a thatched cottage complete with leaded windows and rambling roses. The scale of this cottage would suit a small teapot; for a family-sized one you could add sky and clouds, finishing with blue cord instead of pink around the edge. The finished cover, with its warm interlining, is guaranteed to keep your tea hot while you daydream about a lazy summer in the country.

Size Approximately 18cm × 28cm (7in × 11in), to suit a small teapot.

MATERIALS

33cm × 46cm (13in × 18in) of double-thread 9-gauge canvas
Tapestry needle size 22
Fine-point waterproof felt marker
Rectangular embroidery frame or stretcher
1.3m (1½yd) of 6mm (¼in)

diameter pink cording (made or purchased, see page 44)
30cm (¼yd) of 90cm (36in) wide pink lining fabric
Beige and pink sewing threads
30cm (¼yd) of 90cm (36in) wide medium-weight polyester or cotton wadding

Threads
Anchor stranded cotton: two skeins each of **pink** 35 and 54, **beige** 372 and 376, **green** 842, 887 and 888, **brown** 357, 379 and 380, **grey** 393, **brick** 339,

yellow 302 and 311, **mauve** 104, **black** 403, and **white** 1, and four skeins each of **brown** 368, and **beige** 387

Embroidery stitches
Cross stitch and lattice stitch for the canvaswork and back stitch and herringbone for making up the cosy.

METHOD

▦ Using the felt marker, draw a line across the width of the canvas to divide it into two equal rectangles, one for the front of the teacosy and one for the back. Then draw a vertical line through the centre of each canvas rectangle, taking care not to cross any vertical threads. Mark the central horizontal lines across each rectangle. Rule corresponding lines across the chart to find the centre.
▦ Mount the entire canvas in the embroidery frame or stretcher. On one canvas rectangle, embroider the cottage, starting at the centre of the design and working outwards in cross stitch, following the chart square by square. Use

six strands of thread throughout. Work over the windows in lattice (large herringbone) stitch using the black thread.
▦ Embroider the cottage design again on the remaining canvas rectangle. When all the stitching is completed, block the canvas carefully, following the instructions given on page 15.

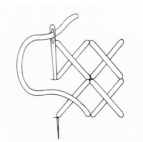

FINISHING

▦ Separate the two embroidered sections and trim away the unworked canvas from both pieces of embroidery, leaving a margin of 2cm (¾in) all around.

▦ Cut two pieces of lining to the same size and shape as the canvas (omitting the chimney tops), and two pieces of wadding 2cm (¾in) smaller all around.

▦ Place the two pieces of embroidery with right sides facing and, using beige thread, backstitch them neatly together, leaving the lower edge open. Turn under the lower edge right up to the embroidery and secure it with a row of herringbone stitch.

▦ Place one piece of wadding over one side of the embroidery, trimming it to the correct shape if necessary. Lay one piece of lining over the wadding and tuck the raw edges neatly between the wadding and the embroidery. Pin the layers in position and then slipstitch the lining neatly to the embroidery, using pink sewing thread. Repeat for the other side of the teacosy.

▦ Turn the teacosy to the right side and hand stitch the cording neatly around the edges as shown on the photograph.

MAKING CORDING

You can either use purchased cording or make your own, with lengths of pink perlé or crochet cotton. First twist strands together to decide how many strands you will need to make 6mm (¼in) diameter cording. To make 1.3m (1½yd) of cording, cut strands 4.1m (4¾yd) long. Put the strands together in one long bunch, with ends level. Tie the bunch in a knot at one end, and slip this end over a hook. Holding the other end of the bunch firmly, twist the strands tightly together. When the entire length is tightly twisted, place one finger at the centre and bring the free ends level with the knotted

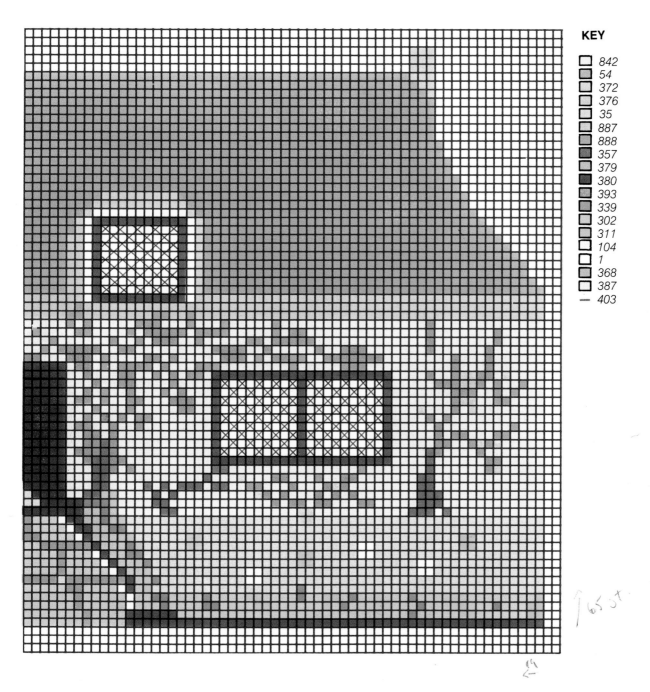

KEY

- 842
- 54
- 372
- 376
- 35
- 887
- 888
- 357
- 379
- 380
- 393
- 339
- 302
- 311
- 104
- 1
- 368
- 387
- — 403

ends. Remove your finger and the strands will twist into a cord. Trim away the first knot and knot all ends together. At the folded end of the cord, make another knot and trim the fold. If desired, use strands of different colours to produce multicoloured cording.

SCATTERED FLOWERS

If you have an old or antique chair which you would like to recover, here is a charming way to do it with the minimum of effort for the maximum of effect: an easy-to-work needlepoint design which takes full advantage of the attractive, neutral tone and interesting texture of embroidery canvas and uses it as the background to a design of tiny, scattered flower sprays. Instead of spending hours and hours filling in a monotone background, you are left with the pleasant task of working the little flowers – if the idea wasn't so successful it would seem like cheating! The instructions explain how to remove the old covers and replace them with the finished needle-point, though you may prefer to let a professional fit the new covers if you do not enjoy upholstery and you are afraid of spoiling the finished work.

Size: to the measure of your existing chair cover.

MATERIALS

Double-thread 10-gauge canvas:
  separate pieces for the front,
  back and seat of the chair
DMC tapestry wool in the
  following colours:
white rose – grey 7321, 7333;
  white; yellow 7431 and 7745;
  orange 7445; green 7320, 7384
pink rose – yellow 7431, 7786;
  pink 7200, 7202, 7204; orange
  7445; green 7362, 7382,
  7542; white
yellow rose – orange 7445;
  yellow 7726, 7727; green
  7369, 7370, 7548, 7584; white
(Quantities are not given as the
  amount required will vary
  according to your chair size
  and the spacing you choose to
  give between flowers.)
Tapestry needle size 18 or 20
Tapestry frame – you could work
  without one, but a frame would
  make stitching easier and
  would help to prevent the
  canvas from becoming
  distorted
Calico (if undercover needs
  replacing)
10mm (⅜in) fine tacks
Two gimp pins
1.5cm (⅝in) wide braid
Curved upholstery needle
Matching thread
Fabric adhesive
Note If the above yarns are
  unobtainable, refer to page 191.

METHOD

▨ Using a wooden mallet and a ripping chisel, remove old back, front and seat covers, easing out old tacks and always working in the direction of the wood grain.
▨ If necessary, add more wadding to the underneath and replace or renew undercover.
▨ Measure the seat both ways and buy canvas to this size, plus at least 20cm (8in) all round. Do the same for inside and outside back.

TAPESTRY

▨ To prevent fraying, bind the canvas edges with masking tape or turn under and stitch a narrow hem.
▨ The motifs are all worked in half cross stitch (see page 13) and each square represents one stitch. Embroider the motifs from the charts, using the photograph as a general guide to positioning. The background is unworked.
▨ As each piece is completed, stretch the canvas back into shape by blocking it: remove binding or holding stitches round edge and if there is a selvedge cut small nicks along it to ensure the canvas can be stretched. Damp the canvas with a wet sponge or a laundry spray.
▨ Take a piece of wood or blockboard larger than the

A
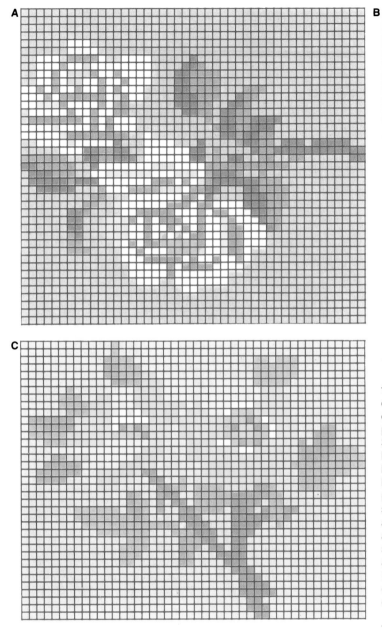

B

C

KEY

A

■	7320
■	7384
■	7333
■	7321
	7745
	7431 *also B*
□	white *also B and C*
■	7445 *also B and C*

B

■	7542
	7382

■	7362
	7786
■	7204
■	7202
	7200

C

■	7584
■	7548
■	7369
■	7370
	7726
	7727

finished embroidery, draw the correct outline of the completed embroidery with a waterproof pen and tape it to the board. Starting at the centre top and bottom of the surplus canvas, lightly tack the canvas to the board, following the marked paper outline. Repeat at the sides, making sure that the warp and weft threads are at right angles. Hammer in tacks securely, then wet the canvas again and leave to dry slowly at room temperature over several days. Repeat as necessary until canvas is restored to shape.

THE COVERING

▦ Place the canvas over the seat and temporarily tack to front and side rails, stretching it taut. Smooth back edge down between back and seat and tack at back of chair to back rail.

▦ At front corners, pull side canvas round to the front rail and tack. Fold excess canvas at the front into a pleat in line with edge of seat (trimming off any excess canvas inside if too bulky). Tack in place. Hand stitch down the folded fabric at each front corner.

▦ Check that the seat is smooth and taut and hammer home all the tacks.

▦ Centre front canvas over chair back and temporarily tack to back of frame at top and sides. Pull lower edge through to the back of the chair and temporarily tack in place. At each side of top, excess canvas will have to be pleated up into small evenly spaced darts – make sure you have the same number of darts at each side. When the darts look right, hammer home the tacks.

▦ Cut calico (or coloured fabric) to fit outside back; centrally place over the back and tack in place inside previous row of tacks.

▦ Centrally place the canvas over calico on outside back, cutting and then turning under the top and side edges, following the lines of the chair and covering over previous tacks; pin in place. Secure lower edge with tacks. Using a curved needle, stitch the side and top edges to the inside back canvas.

▦ Cover tack heads at base with braid. Tack the end in place with a gimp pin, fold braid over tack and stick in place all round the base edge. Secure the opposite end with a gimp pin to finish.

COLOUR AND LIGHT

Even in the middle of winter, this needlepoint mat will give you the feeling of warm sunshine pouring in through a stained glass window, illuminating an intricate pattern of bright, jewel-like colours. The dark outlines, like the leading in a window, enhance the colours until they seem to glow with life. Although the pattern is complex, it is worked on a large-scale canvas, which can be covered quickly.

Size: approximately 80cm × 130cm (32in × 52in).

MATERIALS

1m × 1.5m (1⅛yd × 1⅝yd) of 4-gauge DMC rug canvas
DMC rug wool (uncut) as follows: seven hanks of grey 7333; four hanks of ecru; two hanks each of primrose 7504, blue 7313 and black, and one hank each of gold 7505, blue 7301, 7305, 7307, 7317 and 7326, pink 7120, 7196, 7202 and 7206, beige 7491, green 7347, sand 7520, bronze 7421 and tan 7446 and 7444
Strong button thread
Large tapestry or rug needle
Fine-tip waterproof felt marker
Note If the above yarn is unobtainable, refer to page 191.

METHOD

▦ Draw a vertical line with the marker through the centre of the canvas, taking care not to cross any vertical threads. Mark the central horizontal line in the same way. Rule the corresponding lines across the chart to find the centre of the design.

▦ Bind the edges of the canvas with masking tape to prevent the threads unravelling. Begin stitching at the centre of the canvas, working outwards and following the chart square by square. Each square on the chart represents one half cross stitch.

▦ Embroider the stained glass design first, and then work the black and grey border.

▦ Block the embroidery (see page 15) if it has pulled out of shape during stitching, then trim away the surplus canvas, leaving a margin of 5cm all around the embroidery.

▦ The rug can either be bound with strips of rug binding, as described on page 62, or finished as follows: cutting diagonally across, trim spare canvas from corners to reduce bulk. Fold the canvas to the back at each corner, then bring the side margins to the back to meet at a mitred fold.

▦ Using strong button thread, stitch the sides together along the mitred corners, then secure all edges to the back of the rug with herringbone stitch.

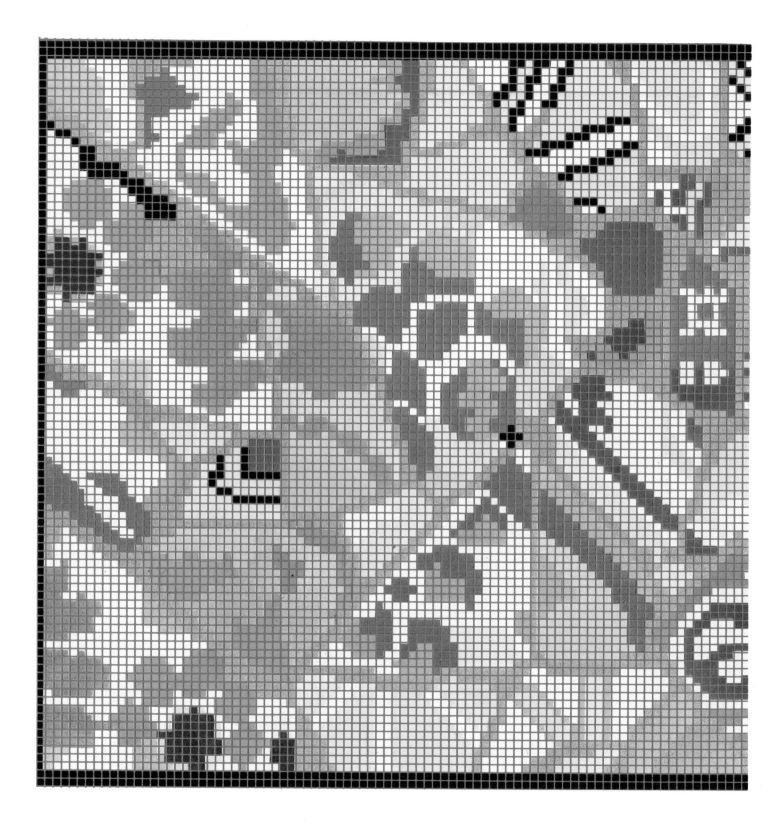

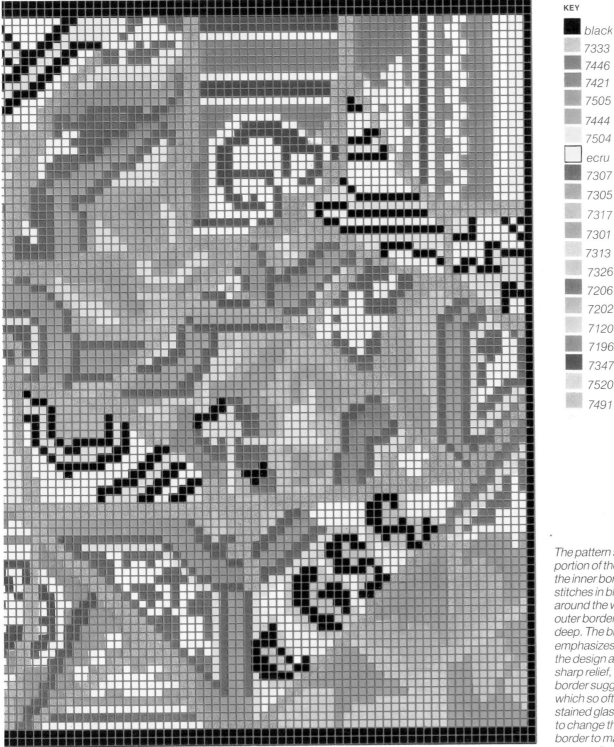

KEY

■	black
	7333
	7446
	7421
	7505
	7444
	7504
□	ecru
	7307
	7305
	7317
	7301
	7313
	7326
	7206
	7202
	7120
	7196
	7347
	7520
	7491

The pattern shows the central portion of the mat. In addition to the inner border of two rows of stitches in black, running all around the work, there is an outer border of grey, seven rows deep. The black inner border emphasizes the bright colours of the design and throws them into sharp relief, while the grey outer border suggests the stone walls which so often surround a stained glass window. If you wish to change the colour of the outer border to match your surroundings, either make a tracing of the design and colour it in, adding the borders, or shade strips of paper in the chosen border colour and frame them round the design.

51

HOLIDAY SOUVENIRS

Practicality and beauty are combined in these two shopping bags, both of which are so pretty that they can be displayed on your kitchen wall when not in use. Alternatively, the designs could be used to make an attractive pair of cushion covers.

Size Each bag measures 39cm × 32.5cm (15½in × 13in).

MATERIALS

FOR ONE BAG

24cm × 32cm (12in × 15in) of single thread 12-gauge canvas
50cm (⅝yd) of 90cm (36in) wide strong linen or cotton fabric in a neutral colour
Matching sewing thread
50cm (⅝yd) of 90cm (36in) wide lining fabric in a neutral colour
Fine-point waterproof felt marker
Rectangular embroidery frame or stretcher
Tapestry needle size 20 or 22

Threads

SEASCAPE BAG
DMC soft embroidery cotton: one skein each of **brown** 2400 and 2829, **grey** 2413, 2414, 2647 and 2933, **black** 2310, **blue** 2595 and 2807, **green** 2502, 2504, 2715 and 2926, and **ochre** 2575 and 2738, and two skeins each of **white**, **grey** 2415 and **green** 2928

MOUNTAIN BAG
DMC soft embroidery cotton: one skein each of **green** 2856, 2926 and 2928, **brown** 2801, **grey** 2233, 2931 and 2933, **beige** 2302, 2543 and 2842, **yellow** 2745, **cream** 2579, **ochre** 2833, and **red** 2304 and 2918, and two skeins each of **white** and **grey** 2415

Embroidery stitches

Both designs are worked in half cross stitch, each square representing one half cross stitch.

METHOD

THE EMBROIDERY

▦ Both pictures are stitched in the same way: start by drawing a vertical line with the felt marker down the centre of the canvas rectangle, taking care not to cross any vertical threads. Mark the central horizontal line in the same way. Rule corresponding lines across the appropriate chart to find the centre of the design.
▦ Mount the canvas in the embroidery frame or stretcher. Begin stitching the design at the centre and work outwards in half cross stitch, following the appropriate chart square by square.
▦ When all the stitching is complete, block the canvas carefully, as explained on page 15.

MAKING THE BAG

▦ Cut out two pieces measuring 42cm × 35.5cm (16¾in × 14¼in) from the main fabric and two pieces the same size from the lining fabric. From main fabric only, cut two strips measuring 7.5cm × 40cm (3in × 16in).
▦ Take one main fabric piece for the front of the bag and, using a pencil, mark out a window for the picture, making it 3cm (1¼in) smaller each way than the dimensions of the embroidered area. The window should be an equal distance from the side and bottom edges of the fabric, and

slightly closer to the top edge.

▦ Cut away the central portion of fabric and turn under an allowance of 1.5cm (⅝in) all around the opening, clipping into the corners so that the fabric will lie flat. Tack the turnings.

▦ Position the fabric over the embroidery and tack in place. Machine stitch around the opening, close to the folded edge.

▦ With right sides facing, pin bag front and back together and machine stitch them together along the sides and bottom edge, taking a 1.5cm (⅝in) seam allowance. Press the seam and turn the bag right side out. Stitch the lining sections together but do not turn them right side out.

▦ Fold each handle strip in half lengthwise, with right sides facing, and machine down the long side, taking a 1cm (⅜in) seam allowance. Turn right side out and press.

▦ Take one handle and position it on the front of the bag, with the raw ends of the handle matching the raw top edge of the bag. The ends should be in line with the side edges of the picture. Stitch across, taking a 1.5cm (⅝in) seam. Stitch the other handle to the back of the bag.

▦ Bringing the handles up, turn under 1.5cm (⅝in) around the top edge of the bag and press. Machine around the three seamed edges of the bag, stitching close to the edge. Turn under and press the raw top edge of the bag lining. Slip it into the bag, then pin and stitch the bag and lining together, machining close to the folded edges.

MOUNTAINEER BAG

KEY

- 2856
- 2926
- 2928
- 2801
- 2233
- 2931
- 2933
- 2302
- 2543
- 2842
- 2745
- 2579
- 2833
- 2304
- 2918
- 2415
- white

SEASCAPE BAG

KEY

- 2400
- 2829
- 2413
- 2414
- 2933
- 2310
- 2595
- 2807
- 2502
- 2504
- 2715
- 2926
- 2575
- 2738
- white
- 2647
- 2415
- 2928

MAJOLICA MAT

A familiar image of the Mediterranean, blue-and-white tiles with their formal, often ornate designs, inspired this idea for a floor mat. Each square is worked separately mainly in cross stitch, then enriched with back stitch and Chinese knots to give the geometric precision of tiles. You have a wealth of designs here to make up as shown, or to adapt for your own ideas – table mats, cushions, chairbacks, folder covers, or a series of framed patterns. If you are ambitious, the mat itself could be enlarged by repeating a combination of the squares.

MATERIALS

20 squares of Pingouin rug canvas, each 50cm (20in) × 50cm (20in)	Large tapestry or rug needle

Threads
Pingouin rug wool: 40 hanks of **white** 05; 15 hanks of **blue** 67; 9 hanks of **blue** 31; 8 hanks of **blue** 65; 7 hanks of **blue** 40; 2 hanks of each of the following colours: **blue** 13, 32, 66, 134; 1 hank of **blue** 28

Embroidery Stitches
Cross stitch, back stitch, Chinese knots, herringbone stitch and half cross stitch.

METHOD

THE CHARTS:

▦ Use chart A for the four corner squares; charts B and C for the ten border squares that make up the garland, and charts 1, 2, 3 and 4 to make up the six central geometric squares: D, E, F, G.

▦ Embroider each square from the appropriate chart. Work squares A, B and C in cross stitch. Work the geometric squares in cross stitch and pick out extra details in back stitch and Chinese knots. Then embroider two rows of back stitch vertically and horizontally across the centre of each square using colour 40.

▦ When all the squares have been embroidered, block each one carefully (see page 15), making sure that they are all the same size: each blocked square should measure 40cm (16in) × 40cm (16in).

▦ Following the arrangement in the diagram, join the squares into four strips of five squares, with flat back-stitched seams. Press the seams open.

▦ Join the strips together in the same way, making sure that the pattern is correct.

▦ On the reverse of the rug, turn in the surplus canvas and secure it with herringbone stitch.

▦ Secure the surplus canvas along each seam in a similar way, using herringbone stitch.

▦ On the top side of the rug, use colour 40 to conceal the seams – work rows of back stitch along them – and to finish the edges off work a row of half cross stitch round the outside of the rug.

Once you have mastered this rug, try using different 'tiles'.

This rug is made up of twenty sections of canvaswork each measuring 40cm (16in) square. Embroider each of the sections systematically from the charts, beginning with the four corner squares which are worked from chart A. Charts B and C are followed to work the ten sections which complete the garland border. The border sections are worked in cross stitch.

The central portion of the rug is made up of six geometrically patterned sections worked in cross stitch, back stitch and Chinese knots. These sections are worked from charts 1, 2, 3 and 4 using different combinations of the pattern charts as shown in the plan.

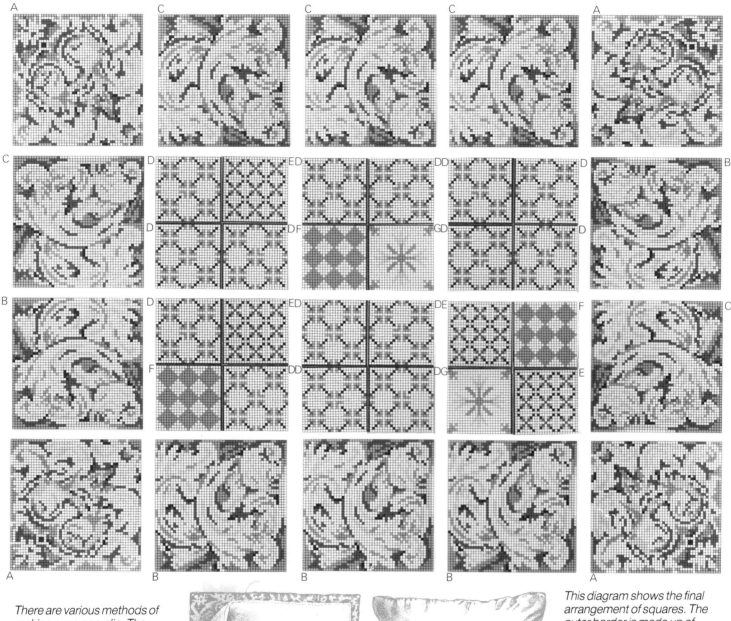

There are various methods of making a rug non-slip. The simplest way is to coat the turned-under edges of the canvas with Copydex rubber solution and leave them to dry thoroughly.

A heavy lining also works well. Cut a piece of hessian slightly larger than the finished rug and turn under the raw edges. Slipstitch the hessian to the wrong side of the rug, as shown in the diagram.

Alternatively, non-slip netting can be purchased. This is cut slightly smaller than the rug and placed between it and the floor.

One section of the rug design can be worked and made into a cushion cover. Finish the edges in the same way as for the pansy bag (see page 40), and slipstitch it to a ready-made cushion cover.

This diagram shows the final arrangement of squares. The outer border is made up of fourteen squares (patterns A, B and C) and the six inner squares are composites, using the four small patterns opposite.

IKEBANA

This square rug, with its interplay of rich autumnal colours and rounded shapes, has a wonderful feeling of life and movement, like a split second taken from a juggling act. It was inspired by an antique Japanese textile, but its simple, almost abstract shapes would blend superbly into an uncluttered modern setting. If these colours are not suited to your decor, trace over the basic outlines and experiment with other colourways until you have found a combination that works. Even a very minor change, such as altering the colour of some balls, perhaps to echo the colour of a lamp base or some scatter cushions, could have a subtle but important effect, bringing the design into harmony with a room setting, without involving a great deal of extra preparation.

Size: approximately 140cm × 140cm (56in × 56in).

MATERIALS

1.5m × 1.5m (60in × 60in) of 4-gauge DMC rug canvas

DMC rug wool in ready-cut packs in the following quantities and colours: 85 packs beige 7143; 66 packs fawn 7520; 30 packs black; 24 packs red 7107; 19 packs pale pink 7120; 8 packs green 7384; 6 packs orange 7850; 5 packs yellow 7504; 4 packs ecru; 3 packs each of blue 7305 and gold 7505, and 2 packs pink 7202

Latchet rug hook

Wide masking tape

6.2m (6⅞yd) of 4cm (1½in) wide rug binding

Heavy duty sewing needle

Beige button thread or linen carpet thread

Note If the above rug yarn is unobtainable, refer to page 191.

METHOD

▦ The rug is knotted using a lachet hook (see overleaf), and each square on the chart represents one rug knot worked over one horizontal thread of canvas.

▦ To make each knot, take a cut strand of wool and fold it in half. Holding the two ends firmly, slip the wool over the hook, below the crook and latch, and insert the hook under a horizontal thread of canvas.

▦ Open the latch and insert the two ends of wool into the hook then closing the latch, pull the ends back under the canvas thread and through the loop.

▦ Pull the two ends to make a firm knot before moving onto the next. If one side of a knot is longer than the other, do not be tempted to trim the longer end as this will result in the finished rug having an uneven pile. Instead, remove the yarn and rework the knot.

▦ Before working the design, bind canvas edges with masking tape to prevent threads unravelling. Work row by row across the canvas, following chart for design and colours. Begin at the lower edge, approximately 12cm in from raw edge of canvas, and work upwards to top of chart, working in horizontal rows. Much of the background of the rug is worked in two colours in order to produce a more interesting, multicoloured pile of either beige and fawn or beige and pink. It is important to stagger the position of the colours from row to row, rather like brickwork, in order to achieve a speckled effect instead of stripes.

▦ When knotting is complete,

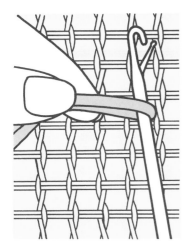

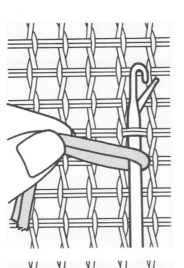

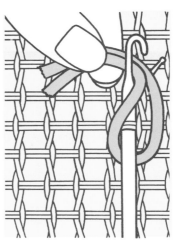

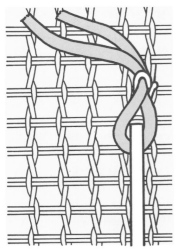

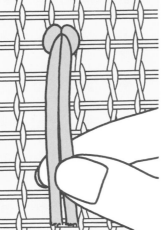

KEY

	7504
	7107
	7202
	7850
	7505
	7384
	7305
	ecru
	7143 alternated with 7520
	7143 alternated with 7120
	black

trim away surplus canvas, leaving a margin of 3cm (1¼in) all around and trimming corners diagonally. Cut the binding into four strips to run the length of the sides and overlap at the corners.

▦ Stitch the binding securely to the rug as shown, keeping the stitching close to the knots. Fold the tape over to the wrong side and slipstitch it in position, mitring the corners.

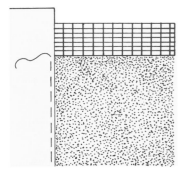

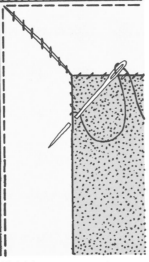

▦ Finish by steam-pressing the completed rug. This will help to set the knots and give the pile a more even, professional appearance. Use a steam iron

and a pressing cloth, such as an old towel or heavy cotton fabric. The rug will be too large to iron easily on an ordinary ironing board, so use a larger surface such as the kitchen table or even the kitchen floor, provided that it is clean and flat. Place the rug face down and cover it with the pressing cloth, which should be damp rather than wet. Iron over the pressing cloth, dampening it again as it dries out, until the entire rug has been ironed. Turn the rug right side up and, again using the pressing cloth, iron on the right side.

▦ There is no need to add a backing: it is better to allow dirt to fall through to the floor.

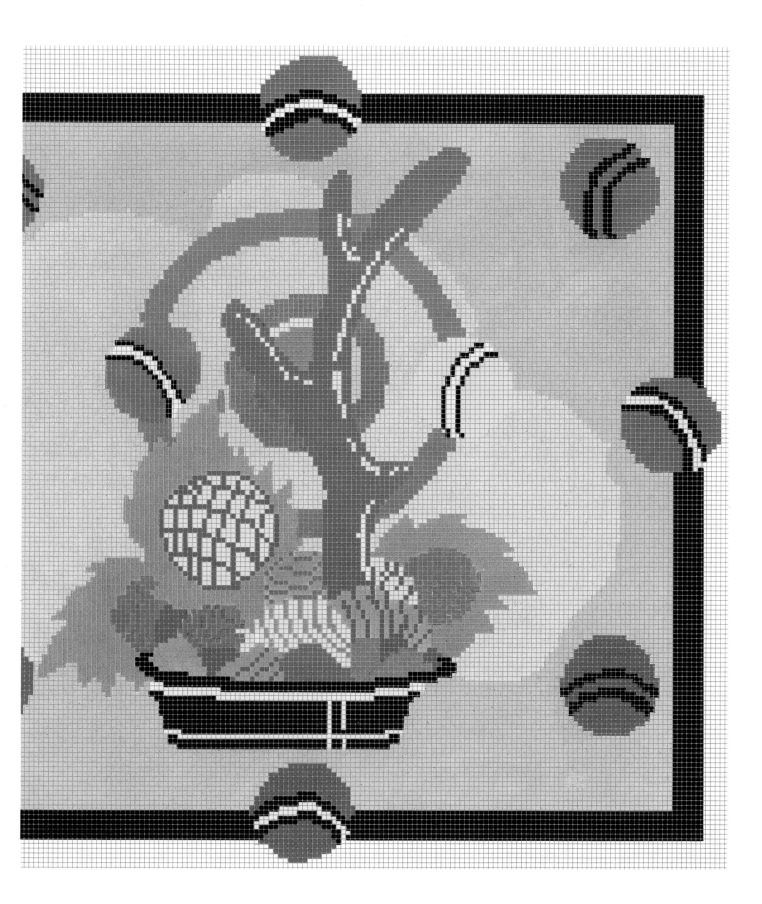

EMBROIDERY FOR YOU

ETHNIC FLOWERS

The brilliant colours of Hungarian floral embroidery have a timeless attraction. The beauty of these flowers is that you can be as ambitious or as small-scale as you like: a plain white dress can be made into a treasured object, or the motifs can be embroidered singly or in clusters for a bag, the front edges of a blouse, for the corner of a shawl or the point of a collar. And they are done simply and quickly in satin stitch and stem stitch. Vary the flower colours to your own taste, but keep them jewel-bright. As with the genuine article, a certain roughness in technique adds life.

MATERIALS

A ready-made garment, or fabric to be made into a shawl, tablecloth or cushion cover.

Crewel needle size 5 or 6
Embroidery hoop

Threads
DMC cotton perle no. 8 in the following shades:
SOLID COLOURS: **green** 703, 704, 895; **yellow** 745, 973; **pink** 352, 818; **orange** 971; **red** 349, 606, 608, 817; **dark red** 815, 902, 3685; **purple** 550
SHADED COLOURS: **green** 122, 126; **blue** 113; **orange** 108; **pink** 99, 112; **red** 57; **mauve** 126

Embroidery Stitches
Satin stitch, stem stitch.

METHOD

▥ Transfer the chosen motifs to the fabric or garment using either the carbon paper method or the transfer pencil method given on page 11.
▥ Work with the fabric or garment stretched in an embroidery hoop, moving the hoop as necessary. If the fabric is very fine or delicate, protect it from damage with a piece of muslin (see page 10).

Using the photograph and diagram on page 68 as colour guides, embroider the flowers and leaves in satin stitch and the stems in stem stitch.
▥ When the embroidery is completed, place it face down on a well-padded surface and press lightly, taking care not to crush the stitches.

The flower motifs can be used to decorate other objects: a box lid (see page 122) or a handkerchief.

The floral designs are intended to be used in an individual way. Be as creative as you like: select single motifs and scatter them over the fabric; mass the flowers closely together to create the riot of colour shown on the previous page; or use just one motif to highlight a garment.

CHORISTERS' COLLARS

These pretty collars in simple cross stitch are detachable, so they can be washed easily and worn with a variety of outfits. By choosing sympathetic colours – grey and yellow, pink and blue, green and turquoise – you can make them to match any favourite dress or smock.

MATERIALS

For each design:	*Crewel needle size 7 or 8*
30cm (12in) × 38cm (15in) Aida even-weave 18-gauge fabric, in white	*Sewing needle*
	5 pairs of small press studs
	1m (1yd) white cotton bias binding
White sewing thread	

Threads
DMC stranded cotton:
1 strand of each: **yellow** *445;*
grey *.318*

Embroidery Stitch
Cross stitch: each square on the charts represents one cross stitch worked over two horizontal and two vertical woven blocks of the fabric.

METHOD

▥ Enlarge the collar pattern to full size on plain paper from the measurements given (see page 10). Check the neckline of the dress to which the collar is to be attached against that of the pattern; adjust if necessary.

▥ Pin the pattern to the fabric and cut out the collar.

▥ Bind the neck edge of the collar with bias binding, as shown in the diagram. Then turn a double 1cm (⅜in) hem around the remaining edges (see page 14 for instructions on mitring corners), pin and hand stitch. Press.

▥ Beginning 2cm (⅝in) above the hem and working from the centre front outwards, embroider the chosen design from the chart in cross stitch. Use three strands of thread throughout.

▥ When the embroidery is completed, place it face down on a well-padded surface and press lightly, taking care not to crush the stitches.

▥ Sew press studs to the collar and dress, placing one pair of studs at the centre fronts, one on each shoulder line, and one at each side of the centre-back opening.

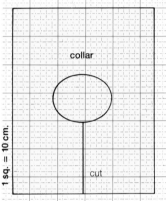

OAK LEAVES AND ACORNS

The couturier Schiaparelli loved creating surreal button designs and these oak leaves and acorns remind one of her inventiveness. Real acorns, threaded through with cord, make unusual buttons, and the acorn motifs embroidered around the buttonholes, on the cuffs, and on the lapels of the dark woollen blazer complement them perfectly.

Sleeve decoration.

Remove the cups from eight acorns and make a hole through each cup. Thread the cord through the hole and make a knot inside the cup. Glue the cup securely on to the acorn before varnishing.

MATERIALS

Ready-made woollen jacket with a fairly smooth weave	Card
16 acorns with cups	Polyurethane varnish
8 short lengths of thin cord in matching or contrasting colours to the embroidery threads	Small paintbrush
	Glue
	White dressmaker's pencil
	Crewel needle size 3 or 4
	Large chenille needle

Threads
DMC stranded cotton:
pale green 368; **dull gold** 834

Embroidery Stitch
Satin stitch.

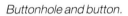

Buttonhole and button.

METHOD

▦ To prepare the acorn 'buttons' thread short lengths of cord through eight acorns, as shown in the diagrams. Remove the cups from the remaining acorns and make a hole through each one as shown. Using a small paintbrush, seal the acorns with the varnish and hang them up to dry; allow twenty-four hours for the varnish to dry thoroughly.

▦ Trace the leaf shapes and transfer them to card. Make a set of templates by carefully cutting round each leaf with a sharp pair of scissors. Using the photographs as a guide, position the templates on the jacket – on the lapels, the edge of the sleeves and round each of the buttonholes – and draw round them with a dressmaker's pencil.

▦ Embroider the leaves in satin stitch using six strands of thread, taking care to cover the guide lines.

▦ Attach the acorn 'buttons' opposite the buttonholes.

▦ Thread each cord of the other set of acorns through the large chenille needle, pull the cords through to the reverse of the jacket and knot each one securely.

PERENNIAL PLEASURES

This rich anemone spray adds individuality and colour to a simple classic jumper. Much easier to achieve than it at first appears, the embroidery is worked on a small piece of fine cotton and then appliquéd on to the jumper in a cunning method that makes the join invisible. You could stitch a floral spray like this – perhaps scaled down – to attach to a velvet or silk cummerbund, to the back of a kimono or a light jacket.

MATERIALS

Ready-made round-necked cotton jumper in pink (the jumper should be of a medium weight to support the embroidery adequately).

40cm (16in) × 30cm (12in) fine white cotton fabric.
Crewel needle size 4 or 5
Embroidery hoop

Threads
DMC stranded cotton:
2 skeins of each of the following colours: SOLID COLOURS: **pink** 600, 601, 602, 603, 604, 605, 754, 818, 819, 948; **yellow** 3078; **green** 320, 730, 734; **red** 606, 666, 815; **blue** 793; **mauve** 554
SHADED COLOURS: **blue** 67, 121, 124; **pink** 48, 62, 112; **mauve** 52, 126; **green** 92, 94

Embroidery Stitch
Long and short stitch with a stitch length of approximately 3 to 4mm.

METHOD

▦ Enlarge the design to the measurements given on the pattern (see page 10). Transfer the design to the fine white cotton using one of the methods given on page 11.
▦ Work with the fabric stretched in an embroidery hoop, moving the hoop as necessary.
▦ Using the photograph and diagram as colour guides, embroider the flowers and leaves in long and short stitch, but leave a narrow area the width of one row of stitches inside the edge of the design. Work with six strands of thread throughout.
▦ When the embroidery is completed apart from the border strip, place it face down on a well-padded surface and press lightly, taking care not to crush the stitches.
▦ Cut away the surplus fabric with a sharp pair of scissors.

▦ Tack the embroidery in place on the jumper. Then work the border strip in long and short stitch, taking the stitches through both the fabric and the jumper and keeping them close together so that the fabric edge is completely covered.

Place the embroidery over the right shoulder as shown.

72

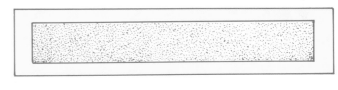

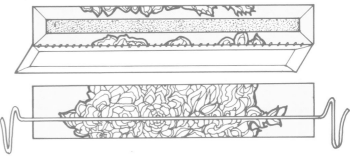

To make the belt shown in the picture above, cut a length of belt stiffening to the correct size and place centrally to the wrong side of the embroidery. Fold the edges of the embroidered fabric over the stiffening, making neat corners. Cut a length of lining to the correct size plus 1.5cm (⅝in) all round. Turn in all edges and hand stitch to wrong side of belt. Hand stitch ribbon centrally to right side.

The design overlaps by 1cm (⅜in) at the centre. Trace the two sections and overlap the tracings to get the complete pattern.

KEY

A	600
B	601
C	602
D	603
E	604
F	605
G	754
H	818
I	819
J	948
K	3078
L	320
M	730
N	734
P	666
Q	815
R	793
S	554
T	67
U	121
V	124
W	48
X	62
Y	112
Z	107
a	52
b	126
c	92
d	94
e	95
f	106
g	606
h	99

The thicker outlines on the design indicate the main shapes, with the thin lines detailing the shading of the interlocking long and short stitches.

The coloured areas on the design will act as a guide to the threads, but refer to the key shown above for the accurate thread numbers.

A POCKETFUL OF FLOWERS

Choose any well-made blouse or shirt and work a little magic to make a flower spray blossom from the pocket. Honeysuckle, bluebells and violets all trail prettily and are simple to embroider.

MATERIALS

Ready-made shirt with a plain patch pocket on the chest 25cm (10in) × 25cm (10in) muslin or fine cotton (if shirt fabric is fine or delicate) Crewel needles sizes 4, 6 and 8 Embroidery hoop

Thread
DMC stranded embroidery cotton in the following shades:
FOR THE BLUEBELLS 1 skein of each:
blue *322, 798, 800, 813;* **green** *368, 369, 502, 504, 966, 989;* **pink** *224, 842;* **yellow** *734*
FOR THE HONEYSUCKLE 1 skein of each:
green *368, 704, 988, 989;* **yellow** *725, 781, 783, 3078;* **pink** *225, 316, 356, 739, 758, 760*
FOR THE VIOLETS 1 skein of each: **green** *368, 937, 966, 988, 989;* **mauve** *and* **pink** *224, 225, 315, 316, 778;* **yellow** *726*

Embroidery Stitches
BLUEBELLS: long and short stitch, satin stitch, stem stitch, straight stitch.
HONEYSUCKLE: long and short stitch, satin stitch, stem stitch, Chinese knots.
VIOLETS: long and short stitch, satin stitch and stem stitch.

METHOD

▦ Transfer the design to the front of the shirt by either the carbon paper or transfer pencil method given on page 11 and positioning it as shown in the photographs. Transfer a single flower to the top of the adjacent sleeve.

▦ If the fabric to be embroidered is fine or delicate, work with both the shirt and the muslin (or cotton) stretched in an embroidery hoop. Cut away the central portion of the muslin to expose the area to be worked. Repeat with a second square of muslin if the design will not fit completely into the hoop, and the hoop needs to be moved.

▦ When working the embroidery use the photographs and diagrams as colour guides.

▦ FOR THE BLUEBELLS, embroider the flowers and leaves in long and short stitch, using satin stitch for the narrow areas. Work the stems of the bluebells and the background foliage in stem stitch, adding groups of straight stitches in pink. Use two strands of thread throughout.

▦ FOR THE HONEYSUCKLE, embroider the flowers and leaves in long and short stitch, using satin stitch for the narrow areas. Work the stems and stamens in stem stitch, and the pistils and pollen in Chinese knots. Use two strands of thread for the flowers, leaves and stems; one strand for the stamens; three strands for the pollen, and six strands for the pistils.

▦ FOR THE VIOLETS, embroider the flowers and leaves in long and short stitch, using satin stitch for the flower centres. Work the stems and leaf veins in stem stitch. Use two strands of thread throughout.

▦ When the embroidery is completed place the shirt face down on a well-padded surface and press lightly, taking care not to crush the stitches.

Bluebell
a 798, b 800, c 813, d 322, *e 989, f 966, g 502, h 504, i 368, j 369, k 842, l 224, m 734*

76

floral detail for a classic blouse

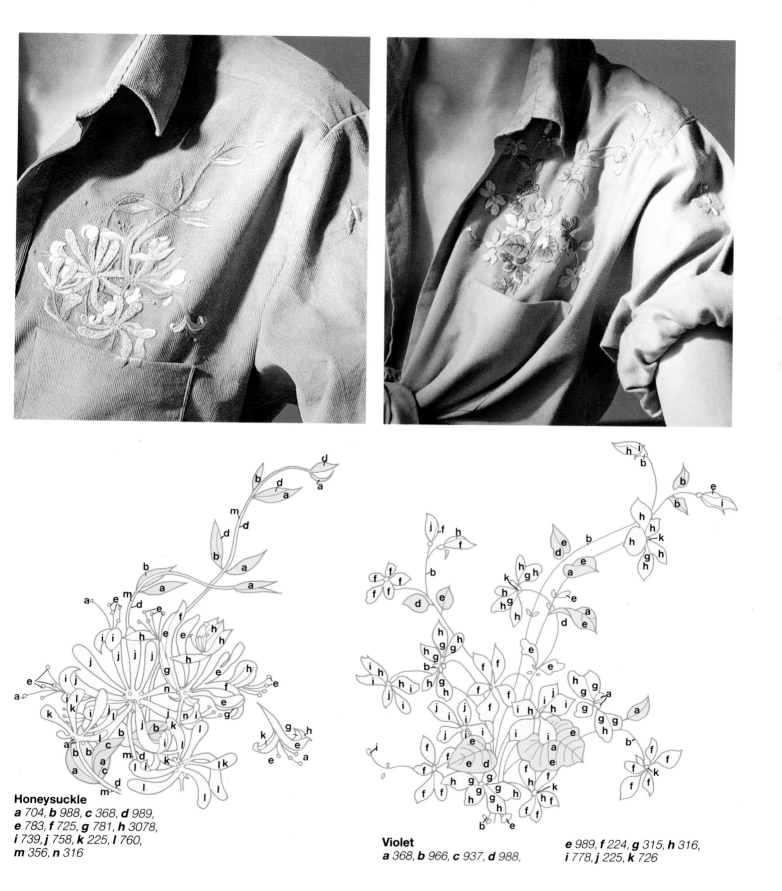

Honeysuckle
a 704, *b* 988, *c* 368, *d* 989,
e 783, *f* 725, *g* 781, *h* 3078,
i 739, *j* 758, *k* 225, *l* 760,
m 356, *n* 316

Violet
a 368, *b* 966, *c* 937, *d* 988,
e 989, *f* 224, *g* 315, *h* 316,
i 778, *j* 225, *k* 726

JUICY FRUITS

Clusters of strawberries or cherries are a perfect decoration for summer whites and pastels – for a dress yoke, a pretty sash or bow, for collars, cuffs, and hemlines. Satin stitch and Chinese knots are quick to embroider and brighten up all sorts of modest everyday objects, such as a tablecloth and napkins or plain kitchen curtains.

MATERIALS

Ribbon and ready-made garment, or household linen	Crewel needle size 4 or 5 Embroidery hoop

Threads
DMC stranded cotton:
THE STRAWBERRIES: **red** 309;
green 911, 954
THE CHERRIES: **red** 321; **green** 909

Embroidery Stitches
Satin stitch, Chinese knots.

METHOD

▦ Transfer the design to the fabric using one of the methods given on page 11.
▦ Work with the fabric stretched in an embroidery hoop.
▦ Embroider the strawberries and leaves in satin stitch using the red and darker green threads, then scatter Chinese knots in the lighter green over the strawberries. Use six strands of thread throughout.
▦ Embroider the cherries, stalks and leaves in satin stitch, using six strands of thread throughout.
▦ When the embroidery is completed, place it face down on a well-padded surface and press lightly, taking care not to crush the stitches.

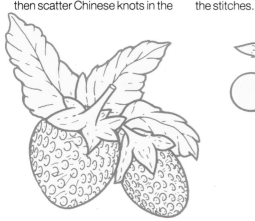

Embroider these strawberry and cherry motifs to add a touch of summer to clothes and household linen. They look best worked on a white or pale-coloured background to show off the bright red and green of the threads. Use them singly, scattered at random, or in neat rows to make an unusual border pattern.

To place the strawberries in the correct position, first tie the ribbon into the desired shape bow. Then mark where the strawberries would look best on the ribbon. Untie the ribbon carefully and mark out the design and embroider it.

BABY ALPHABET

Straight out of Kate Greenaway, this alphabet layette will be a childhood treasure. The skilled embroiderer can make a quilt for the cot; those less patient could use the appropriate initials to add a little colour and individuality to the simplest baby clothes. The letters are formed in padded satin stitch, while the charming figures are easy to copy in long and short stitch. Use shop-bought pillow cases or quilt covers if you prefer, but remember wadded fabric will not fit into your embroidery hoop.

MATERIALS

1m (1yd) × 1m (1yd) of white cotton or linen for the cover	pillowcase
Ready-made baby cotton or linen	Crewel needle size 6 or 7
	Embroidery hoop

Threads

DMC stranded cotton (the colours are given below each diagram and are the ones used for the alphabet in the photograph, but you could substitute other colours if you prefer)

MAIN PART OF LETTERS: **turquoise** 807

FACES, ARMS AND LEGS: **flesh pink** 754

CHEEKS: **pink** 761

Embroidery Stitches

Padded satin stitch, back stitch, horizontal long and short stitch, straight stitch.

METHOD

▦ Enlarge the design to the desired dimension. Transfer the complete alphabet to the square of white fabric using one of the methods given on page 11 and placing it centrally. Transfer two letters to the top corners of the pillowcase, using the photograph as a guide to the placement.

▦ Using the close-up photographs as a guide to the way stitches are used and the diagrams as colour guides, embroider the letters in padded satin stitch with back stitch for the narrow areas. Embroider the figures in horizontal long and short stitch, with straight stitch and back stitch for the outlines, stripes and tiny details. Work with three strands of thread throughout.

▦ When the embroidery is completed, place it face down on a well-padded surface and press lightly, taking care not to crush the stitches.

▦ Turn a narrow hem round the cot cover (see page 14 for instructions on mitring corners) and machine or hand stitch.

Embroider the letters first and then the solid areas of the figures. Lastly, pick out the outlines, stripes and tiny details to give definition.

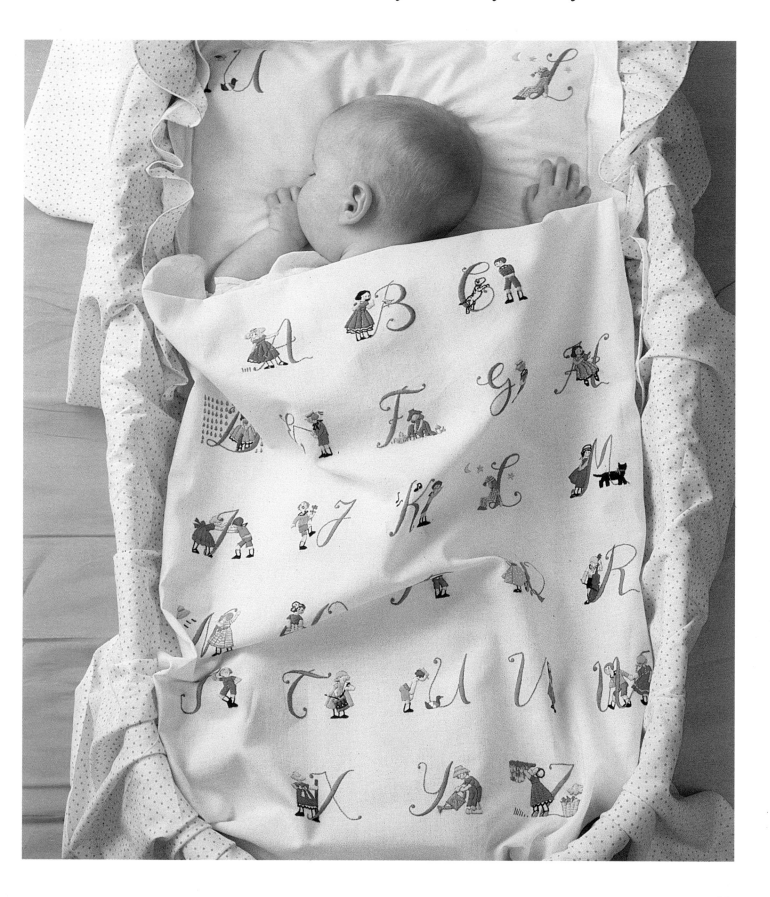

LETTER A: **pink** 957, **yellow** 726, **green** 320, **pink** 3350, **black** 310, **purple** 208

LETTER B: **black** 310, **pink** 3350, **green** 912, **yellow** 726, **blue** 927, **red** 321

LETTER C: **black** 310, **red** 321, **brown** 400, **blue** 826, **purple** 208, **pink** 957

LETTER D: **blue** 927, **brown** 400, **purple** 208, **pink** 957, 3350, **gold** 783, **black** 310

LETTER I: **purple** 208, **turquoise** 806, **yellow** 726, **black** 310, **brown** 400, **pink** 3350, **coral** 351, **green** 954, 320

LETTER J: **tan** 976, **black** 310, **green** 954, **blue** 826, **red** 350

LETTER K: **black** 310, **brown** 400, **tan** 976, **pink** 957, 3350, **blue** 826

LETTER L: **red** 350, **turquoise** 807, **blue** 828, **tan** 976, **yellow** 726

LETTER O: **blue** 826, 828, **brown** 400, **pink** 3350, **flesh pink** 754, **blue** 927, **yellow** 725, **black** 310

LETTER P: **black** 310, **blue** 826, **purple** 208

LETTER Q: **blue** 826, **pink** 957, **gold** 783, **fawn** 613, **black** 310, **white**

LETTER R: **yellow** 726, **green** 954, **brown** 400, **black** 310, **cream** 712

LETTER U: **brown** 400, **coral** 351, **yellow** 725, **cream** 712, **black** 310, **blue** 930, **green** 912, 954

LETTER V: **yellow** 726, **red** 320, **black** 310, **blue** 826, **pink** 3350

LETTER W: **tan** 976, **green** 954, **pink** 957, 3350, **black** 310, **purple** 208

LETTER X: **yellow** 726, **blue** 826, **pink** 3350, **brown** 400, **white**

LETTER E: **red** 321, 350, **blue** 828, **black** 310, **tan** 976, **green** 912, **gold** 783, **yellow** 726

LETTER F: **pink** 3350, **blue** 826, **tan** 976, **yellow** 725, 726, **green** 320, **fawn** 613, **cream** 712, **black** 310

LETTER G: **yellow** 726, **red** 350, **gold** 783, **purple** 208, **fawn** 613, **black** 310

LETTER H: **brown** 400, **red** 350, **pink** 3350, **green** 954, **black** 310, **white**

LETTER M: **pink** 3350, **black** 310, **purple** 208, **blue** 826

LETTER N: **yellow** 725, 726, **coral** 351, **black** 310, **green** 954, **gold** 783, **white**

Applying the motifs

Embroidered letters are an unusual but effective way to personalize clothes and household items, and these letters applied individually will look particularly stylish on baby's toys and clothes. Make sure that Teddy does not wander by marking his T-shirt. A simple bib or baby suit can be given a touch of individuality with the first letter of the owner's name embroidered in a prominent place. And, if you do not have the time to embroider the complete alphabet on a baby quilt, simply embroider baby's name or initials.

LETTER S: **tan** 976, **purple** 208, **red** 350, **black** 310, **turquoise** 806

LETTER T: **black** 310, **red** 321, **green** 954, **pink** 957, **yellow** 726, **blue** 826, **cream** 712

LETTER Y: **yellow** 725, **gold** 783, **coral** 351, **blue** 826, 927, **purple** 208

LETTER Z: **yellow** 725, 726, **red** 321, **green** 320, 369, **turquoise** 806, **black** 310, **purple** 208, **gold** 783, **brown** 400

BEETLE BACKS

Little monsters with shiny exotic wings are a wittier decoration to wear on your sleeve than a tender heart! They look all the better for advancing in a cluster: simple satin and straight stitch make them easy to embroider. The designs were copied straight from a book on insects – why not explore studies on fauna for some other unusual motifs? With luck you can find a subject just the right size and trace directly over it for your transfer.

MATERIALS

Ready-made white cotton shirt
  with short sleeves
Crewel needle size 7 or 8

Small piece of stiff card
Embroidery hoop

Threads
DMC stranded cotton as
indicated below each beetle.

Embroidery Stitches
Satin stitch, straight stitch.

METHOD

▨ Enlarge the designs to the desired dimension. Place the piece of card in the sleeve to protect the under-sleeve and transfer the design to the fabric using the carbon paper method given on page 11. Then remove the card.

▨ Work with the fabric stretched in an embroidery hoop, moving the hoop as necessary.

▨ Using the photographs and diagrams as colour guides, embroider each beetle body in satin stitch and the antennae and narrow parts of the legs in straight stitch. Use two strands of threads throughout.

▨ When the embroidery is completed, place it face down on a well-padded surface and press lightly, taking care not to crush the stitches.

BEETLE 1: **yellow** 742, 747; **green** 943, 991; **blue** 807

BEETLE 2: **yellow** 307, 726; **ochre** 783; **brown** 434; **black** 310

BEETLE 3: **red** 355; **green** 943, 991; **brown** 301; **ochre** 783

BEETLE 4: **green** 704, 943, 991; **yellow** 727; **brown** 801

BEETLE 5: **yellow** 744, 783; **black** 310; **chestnut** 976

BEETLE 6: **yellow** 472; **black** 310; **ochre** 729

BEETLE 7: **red** 666; **black** 310; **yellow** 727

BEETLE 8: **orange** 741; **brown** 3371; **red** 349; **ochre** 729

EMBROIDERY FOR YOUR HOME

STRAWBERRY FAIR

Tendrils of wild strawberries make a perfect border for a white tablecloth, set for summer. They have the restrained prettiness of an Edwardian, hand-painted watercolour. Chinese knots are used for the berry seeds over satin stitch, in subtle blends of colour.

MATERIALS

One plain white tablecloth with a fine, smooth weave, preferably in pure cotton. If a square cloth is used it should measure at least 165cm (5ft 6in) across to allow for one complete spray to be worked along each side. If you prefer a rectangular cloth, the length should be at least 137cm (4ft 6in) to accommodate one complete spray along each long side.
Crewel needle size 7 or 8
Embroidery hoop

Threads
DMC stranded cotton
Flowers: **pink** 819, 3689; **gold** 676; **green** 954
Strawberries: **red** 321, 498, 815; **white**
LEAVES 1: **green** 367, 989; veins – **green** 319
LEAVES 2: **gold** 834; **green** 3013; veins – **dull green** 3053

Embroidery Stitches
Long and short stitch, encroaching satin stitch, satin stitch, Chinese knots, stem stitch.

METHOD

☐ Enlarge the design on page 90 to the measurements given on the pattern. Transfer it to the cloth using one of the methods given on page 11.

▦ Work with the cloth stretched in an embroidery hoop, moving the hoop along the cloth as each portion is completed, and use three strands of the thread.

▦ To embroider the flowers, work one row of long and short stitch in the deep pink along the edge of the petals. Fill in the petals using the light pink and the same stitch until the centre circle is reached.

▦ Mass Chinese knots in yellow to make the raised centre and work the small leaves between the petals in green satin stitch.

▦ Embroider the strawberries in encroaching satin stitch in three shades of red: use the darkest red to outline the shape, and then fill in towards the centre, shading the fruit from dark to light.

▦ Scatter tiny white Chinese knots over this stitching.

▦ Work the calyx in satin stitch using either green or gold, as shown on the pattern.

▦ Embroider the leaves in shades of green (leaves 1) or gold (leaves 2), as indicated on the pattern. Work a row of encroaching satin stitch in the darker colour round the edge of the leaf and then fill in the remainder using the same stitch and the lighter colour.

▦ Work the veins in stem stitch.

▦ Embroider the stalks in stem stitch using one strand of each green used on leaf 1 to make up a three-strand thread.

▦ When the embroidery is complete, place the cloth face down on a well-padded surface and press lightly, taking care not to crush the stitches.

The flower and strawberry are shown life-size. Use them as a guide for blending the colours from dark to light. They also show the stitches which are used for each motif.

delicious berries for summer settings

Use the leaf diagrams as a guide to blending the different colours of encroaching satin stitch. Leaf 1 is in three shades of green and leaf 2 is in green mixed with gold.

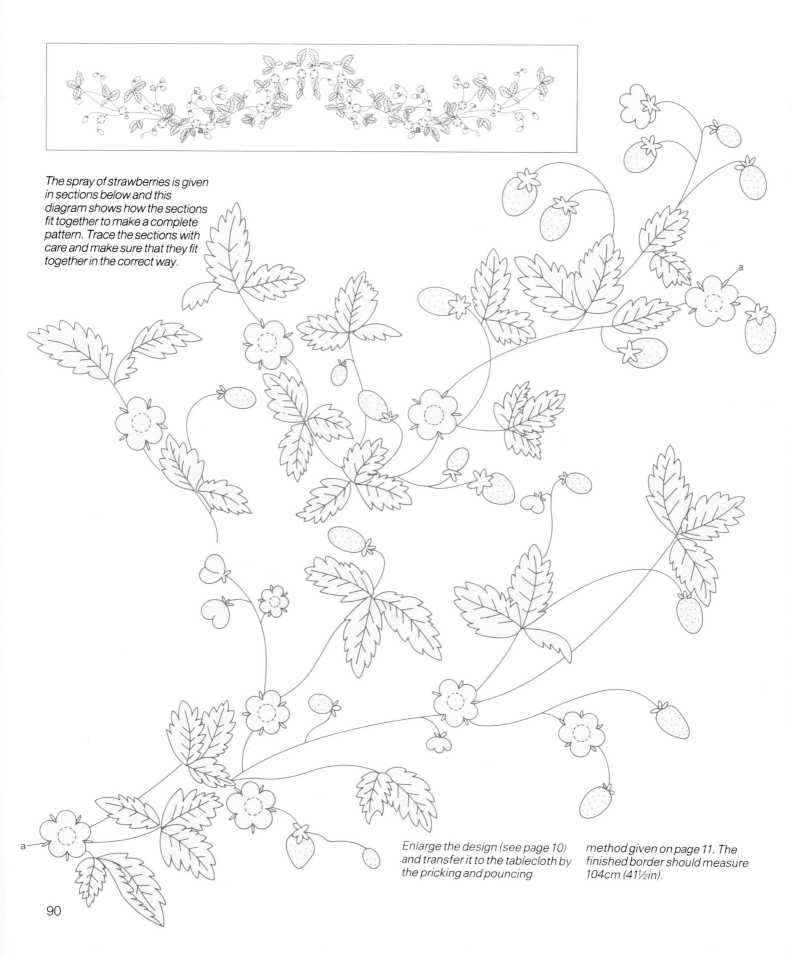

The spray of strawberries is given in sections below and this diagram shows how the sections fit together to make a complete pattern. Trace the sections with care and make sure that they fit together in the correct way.

Enlarge the design (see page 10) and transfer it to the tablecloth by the pricking and pouncing method given on page 11. The finished border should measure 104cm (41½in).

RUG TRANSFORMATION

If you are looking for something to brighten a corner of your room without going to enormous effort or expense, here is a comparatively quick way of adding your personal touch to a plain rug or mat and transforming it with a trelliswork and some scattered flowers. This simple pattern can easily be adapted to any size of rug, either by altering the scale or by simply extending the trellis in either direction, perhaps adding more random flowers.

Size: approximately 100cm × 190cm (40in × 76in), for quantities given.

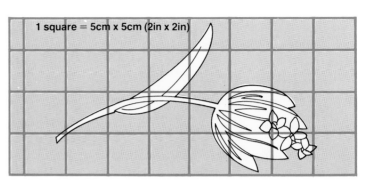

MATERIALS

Woven rug in cotton or wool
Pingouin yarns in the following quantities and colours: Iceberg – two balls yellow 473 and one ball black 41; Pingostar – two balls grey 512 and one ball dark blue 528; Pingoland – one ball each of dark pink 822 and red 831; Tapis – one ball each of kingfisher 60 and emerald

35; Confortable sport – one ball bright pink 33
Large chenille needle
Tracing paper
Dressmakers' carbon paper
20cm × 1m (8in × 40in) strip of stiff card
Fine-tipped waterproof felt marker

METHOD

▣ On the reverse of the rug, mark a trellis of diagonal lines 20cm (8in) apart with the marker, using the strip of card as a guide.

▣ Enlarge the single flower pattern on tracing paper and, using dressmakers' carbon paper and turning the flower tracing different ways, transfer the complete pattern of scattered flowers to the right side of the rug.

▣ Embroider the flowers and leaves in long and short stitch and the grey stems and black pistils in overcast stitch as shown below, using the photograph as a colour and stitch guide.

▣ Following the lines marked on the reverse of the rug, embroider the diagonal black lines in darning stitch, keeping each stitch approximately 1cm (⅜in) long.

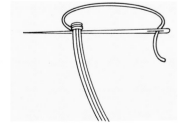

CYPRESS, PALM AND PINE

Embroidered pictures so often look ornate and out of keeping with modern interiors. But these tree specimens have the delicacy of botanical prints, burnished with a southern sunset. Use a fine, sand-coloured linen as a sympathetic background, and mount the studies simply between sheets of perspex.

MATERIALS

55cm (22in) × 55cm (22in) linen or cotton fabric in a neutral colour for each tree

Crewel needle size 6 or 7
Large embroidery hoop

Threads
DMC stranded cotton – 1 skein in each of the following colours:
THE PALM TREE: **brown** *433, 938, 3045;* **green** *470, 472, 500, 890, 987*
THE CYPRESS TREE: **brown** *940, 3032, 3371;* **mauve** *413;* **green** *500, 502, 503, 504, 924*
THE PINE TREE: **green** *500, 580, 732, 937*

Embroidery Stitches
PALM TREE: satin stitch, straight stitch, long and short stitch.
CYPRESS AND PINE TREES: long and short stitch.

METHOD

▨ Enlarge the design to the measurements given on the pattern. Transfer the design to the fabric using one of the methods given on page 11.
▨ Work with the fabric stretched in a large embroidery hoop, moving the hoop as necessary.
▨ Using the diagrams as a colour guide, embroider the palm tree in satin stitch and long and short stitch for the trunk, and straight stitch for the fronds.

Using the close-up photograph as a guide, embroider the cypress and pine trees in long and short stitch. Use three strands of thread throughout.
▨ When the embroidery is completed, place it face down on a well-padded surface and press lightly, taking care not to crush the stitches.
▨ The pictures can be framed with a surround, or mounted very simply between two sheets of perspex as shown in the photograph.

Frame the embroidery between two sheets of perspex clipped together. A small strip of double-sided tape can be used on the back of each corner to hold the embroidery in place.

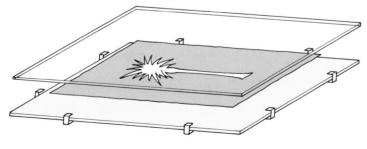

Cypress
a	504
b	503
c	502
d	924
e	413
f	500
g	3371
h	840
i	3032

Palm
a	472
b	987
c	470
d	890
e	500
f	433
g	938
h	3045

Pine
a *732*
b *580*
c *937*
d *500*
e *938*
f *869*
g *780*
h *434*

TROPICAL PARADISE

Size 144cm × 144cm (56in × 56in).

MATERIALS

1.5m × 1.5m (58½in × 58½in) of black cotton or cotton/linen fabric (the motifs are placed at random, so it does not matter if you choose to change the dimensions slightly)

Black sewing thread
Crewel needle size 3 or 4
Dressmakers' carbon paper in a light colour
Large embroidery hoop

Threads

*DMC Soft Embroidery Cotton: one skein each of **yellow** 2741 and 2743, **blue** 2597, 2599, 2797, 2798 and 2807, **grey** 2415, **green** 2347, 2595, 2788, 2952, 2954, 2956, 2957, 2905 and 2909, **orange** 2740, 2742, 2946 and 2947, **pink** 2351 and 2892, **red** 2349, **violet** 2209, **brown** 2299 and 2839, and two skeins each of **yellow** 2307 and 2745, **blue** 2826, and **grey** 2318*

Embroidery stitches

Encroaching satin stitch, straight stitch, stem stitch and Chinese knots.

13

96

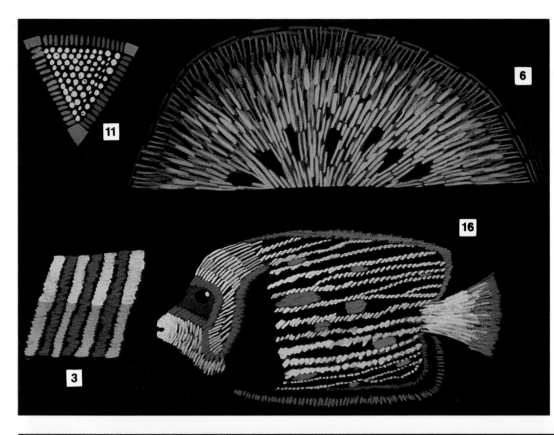

METHOD

▦ Trace the outlines of the motifs, all of which are shown half size, and enlarge them to the required dimensions, as shown on page 10. You will probably find it easier to fill in the minor details by hand, or to 'paint' them directly with your needle.

▦ Using the photograph as a general guide to position, transfer the outlines to the fabric, using dressmakers' carbon paper.

▦ Work with the fabric stretched in the embroidery hoop and re-position it as necessary. Embroider the motifs, using the photographs as stitch and colour guides.

▦ When the embroidery is completed, place the fabric face down on a well-padded surface and press it lightly, taking care not to crush the stitches.

▦ Turn under a double 1.5cm (⅝in) hem along each edge of the square of fabric, mitring the corners, and hem by hand. Press the hem.

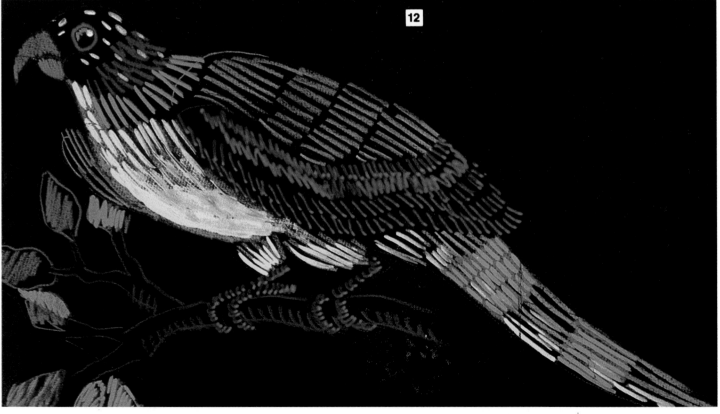

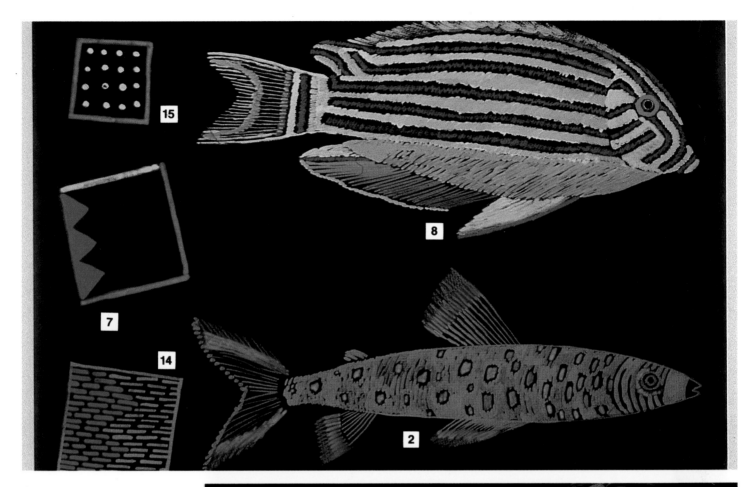

Colours used for each motif
1 2307 and 2956
2 2318, 2946 and 2347
3 2743, 2741 and 2826
4 2798 and 2957
5 2743, 2954 and 2351
6 2892, 2351, 2595, 2952 and 2954
7 2349 and 2892
8 2742, 2741, 2743, 2788, 2826, 2318 and 2415
9 2957, 2349 and 2798
10 2788, 2947, 2740 and 2742
11 2307, 2826, 2318, 2349 and 2209
12 2307, 2745, 2599, 2597, 2797, 2957, 2349, 2299 and 2839
13 2956, 2905 and 2909
14 2798 and 2318
15 2946 and 2307
16 2307, 2745, 2798, 2807, 2415 and 2299

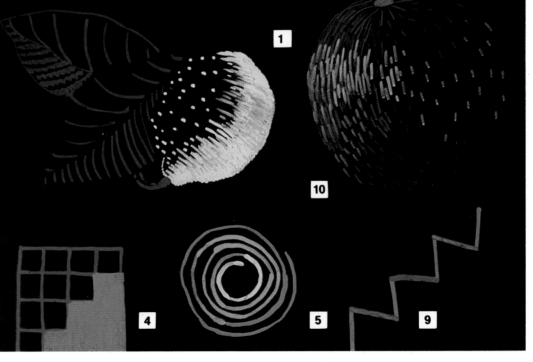

RAFFIA AND FLOWERS

Richelieu work, traditional European embroidery, surfaces in a novel and simplified form in these embroidered mats. Some of the leaves and flowers use rainbow-coloured threads, the shaded colours appearing at random.

MATERIALS

Circular or oval woven raffia tablemats	Chenille needle size 24 Glue and spreader

Threads
DMC stranded cotton in the following colours:
yellow 307, 973; **pink** 603, 605, 718; **red** 321, 606, 815; **mauve** 553; **green** 699, 904, 906; **blue** 792, 703, 704; **shaded green** 123, 124; **shaded pink** 116; **shaded yellow** 104; **black** 310

Embroidery Stitches
Buttonhole stitch, long and short stitch, straight stitch.

METHOD

▣ Trace off the designs from the photograph and enlarge them to fit the mats (see page 10). Transfer the design to the mats using the carbon paper method given on page 11.

▣ To prevent the raffia from fraying when the edges are cut, spread a thin film of glue over the narrow areas of the design and the edges of the flowers and leaves, keeping the glue 3mm (⅛in) inside the edges of the design. Leave the mats to dry thoroughly.

▣ Cut away the areas of raffia which are indicated on the design using a sharp pair of scissors.

▣ Use the photograph as a colour and stitch guide and work with six strands of thread throughout. Embroider the leaves, joining strips and mat edges in buttonhole stitch and keep the stitches close together to completely cover the raffia beneath.

▣ Edge the flowers in closely worked buttonhole stitch, but with the uprights of the stitches irregularly sized.

▣ Fill in the centres of the flowers with long and short stitch, and pick out the leaf veins with straight stitch.

Trace the design from this guide, then enlarge it to fit the size of your raffia mats (see page 10).

NATURE OBSERVED

Sunday in the country, French style, requires an elegantly packed picnic feast, complete with a freshly laundered tablecloth of enormous charm. The cloth is scattered with fruit, nuts, seed heads and insects, the latter so meticulously observed and so lifelike that they might just have jumped on to share the feast. Some 31 colours are used to create this gem of botanical accuracy, but the result is so delightful that it is well worth the attention to detail and the extra effort involved.

Size 192cm × 232cm (77in × 91½in).

MATERIALS

2.4m (2⅝yd) of 200cm (80in) wide fine cream linen or cotton fabric	Dressmakers' carbon paper
	Crewel needle size 6 or 7
	Large embroidery hoop
Matching sewing thread	

Threads
DMC stranded cotton: one skein each of **brown** 435, 632, 898 and 3064, **green** 367, 471, 472, 734, 3051 and 3053, **yellow** 676, 726 and 3078, **blue** 826, **gold** 783 and 3045, **turquoise** 991, **rust** 918, **tan** 781, **beige** 822 and 3047, **cream** 712, **red** 350 and 498, **grey** 642, **white** and **black**

Embroidery stitches
Satin stitch, long and short stitch and stem stitch.

METHOD

▦ Trace the motifs, which are shown full size.

▦ Using the photograph as a guide to position, transfer the motifs to the fabric with dressmakers' carbon paper.

▦ Work with the fabric stretched in the embroidery hoop, re-positioning it as necessary. Embroider the motifs mainly in satin stitch and long and short stitch, picking out the details in stem stitch. Use the close-up photograph as a stitch and colour blending guide.

▦ Embroider the grasses, bee, small yellow insect and small blue insect using two strands of thread in the needle. Complete the rest of the design using three strands of thread throughout.

▦ When the embroidery is finished, place the fabric face down on a well-padded surface and press it lightly, taking care not to crush the stitches.

▦ Turn under a double 2cm (¾in) hem all around the fabric and hem by hand. Press the hem.

long and short stitch

stem stitch

KEY

350
498
918
898
632
435
3064
781
783
726
676
3078
3047
3045
822
712
3051
367
471
472
3053
734
826
991
642
black
white

HOLIDAY FUN CURTAIN

This bright, cheerful door curtain, an effective screen between a cool interior and the blazing sun outside, is made by threading colourful strips of bias binding through the open mesh of the net. It's so easy that even a child could do it, instantly turning a utilitarian screen into something festive and informal, happily at home with cottage flowers and sunny summer days.

Size: made to fit your door or window space.

MATERIALS

Heavy cotton netting with an open mesh (the holes should be distributed in a regular pattern and large enough to hold the folded tape easily)
2.5cm (1in) wide bias binding in green, yellow, red, pink, violet, blue and black (market stalls are often a cheap source)
10cm (4in) wide white fringing for lower edge
Bodkin for threading
Matching thread

METHOD

▦ Measure the door or window opening and cut fabric to this size, adding 10cm (4in) to the width for side hem allowances plus ease, and a sufficient allowance to the length for the desired finish at the top edge.
▦ Turn under a double 1.5cm (⅝in) hem down both side edges; pin, tack and stitch.
▦ Turn up lower edge of curtain to right side for 1cm (⅜in); pin and tack. Position fringing over turned-up edge, turning in the outer edges, in line with side hems. Pin, tack and topstitch fringing in place.
▦ Finish the top edge of the curtain in the desired way.
▦ Using pins, mark the position of the design, about one design width from lower edge. The spacing will depend to some extent on the length of the curtain, but it would be better to have more plain curtain above the design than below.
▦ Thread a manageable length – about 40cm (16in) – of binding through the bodkin, folding the binding in half widthways, with raw edges inside. Following the diagram for colours and pattern, weave the bodkin in and out through the natural gaps in the fabric. Cut the binding at the end of each line of the design, leaving loose ends of equal length – about 1cm (⅜in) at either end.
Note The curtain can either be finished at the top with ordinary curtain tape (which would then be left ungathered) and hung from a curtain rail or pole, or you could make a casing at the top and thread this over a dowel or pole.

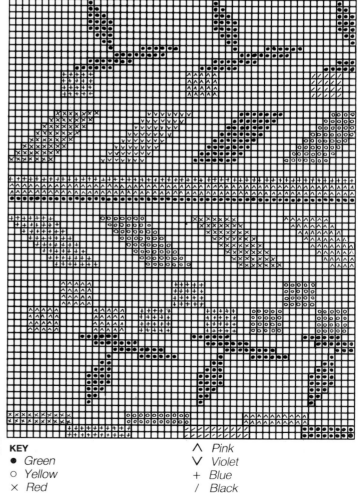

KEY

●	Green	∧	Pink
○	Yellow	∨	Violet
✕	Red	+	Blue
		/	Black

106

CHARACTER NAPKIN

The ultimate refinement for a table set with traditional blue-and-white porcelain ware, this napkin decorated with drawn-threadwork and Chinese characters worked in padded satin stitch will add to the authenticity of any Chinese meal.

Size 16¾in × 16¾in (42cm × 42cm).

MATERIALS

45cm × 45cm (18in × 18in) square of fine white even-weave cotton or linen fabric
Crewel needle size 6 or 7

Dressmakers' carbon paper in a dark colour
Embroidery hoop

Threads
DMC stranded cotton: one skein each of **blue** 798 and **white**

Embroidery stitches
Padded satin stitch for the motifs and hem stitch for the border.

METHOD

BORDER EMBROIDERY
▦ Withdraw sufficient threads to make a narrow border round the square of fabric, approximately 2.5cm (1in) from the raw edge. Neaten the drawn corners by threading short lengths of the strands back into the fabric.
▦ Turn under 6mm (¼in) and then turn a hem so that the fold is just below the edge of the border. Mitre the corners (page 14), and pin and tack the hem in place.
▦ Work a row of hem stitching to secure the hem using three strands of the white thread. Take each stitch round a group of three or four threads, depending on the weight of fabric being used. Repeat the hem stitching at the other side of the border to make a ladder pattern. Press the hem.

MOTIF EMBROIDERY
▦ Trace off the Chinese character motifs. Using the photograph as a guide to position, transfer the motifs to the napkin using the carbon paper method described on page 11. Stretch the napkin in the embroidery hoop.
▦ Begin the embroidery by forming the padding for the satin stitch. Do this by filling the outlined shapes with close lines of back stitch, using two strands of thread in the needle. Work the back stitch down the length of the shapes, rather than across them.
▦ Finish the embroidery by working satin stitch across the lines of back stitch, using four strands of thread. When the embroidery is finished, place the napkin down on a well-padded surface and press it lightly, taking care not to crush the stitches.

hem stitch

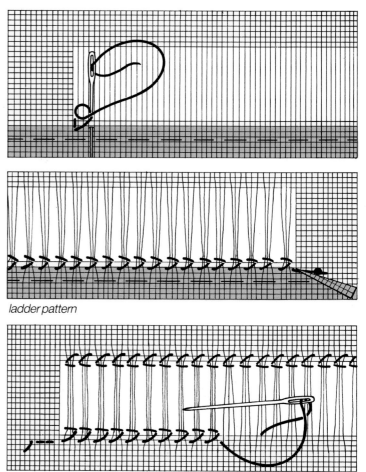

ladder pattern

MEDITERRANEAN GARLAND

That occasional chair which fills an unused corner can become an appealing conversation piece with just a little thought. A garland of mimosa, poppies, wild roses, carnations, fuchsias, orange blossom and oleander, with its attendant butterfly and ladybirds, twines around the edge of a drop-in chair seat. To give the appearance of an all-over tapestry cover – with none of the hard work – a patterned damask brocade is used, its geometric pattern cleverly offsetting the summer blooms.

MATERIALS

Piece of upholstery-weight fabric. To calculate the amount measure the width of your chair, from side to side and back to front, and add 5cm (2in) to each measurement.
Crewel needle size 5 or 6
Embroidery hoop

Threads
DMC stranded cotton – 1 skein of each of the following colours: **ecru** and **white**; **pink** 223, 224, 225, 316, 605, 778, 818, 819, 3688, 3689; **green** 320, 367, 471, 502, 503, 504, 912, 3053, 3347, 3348; **red** 325, 350; **coral** 351; **turquoise** 578; **gold** 676; **yellow** 725, 727, 742, 743, 744, 745, 3078; **bronze** 734; **peach** 754, 945, 951; **beige** 739; **blue** 828, 3325; **blue/grey** 927, 928

Embroidery Stitches
Satin stitch, long and short stitch, seed stitch, stem stitch, padded satin stitch.

METHOD

▦ Enlarge the design to fit the chair seat (see page 10). Transfer the design to the fabric using the carbon paper method given on page 11, positioning the garland centrally on the fabric.

▦ Work with the fabric in an embroidery hoop, moving the hoop as necessary. Using the photograph and diagram as guides, embroider the flowers and leaves in satin stitch and long and short stitch, and pick out the details at the centre of the flowers with seed stitch. Work the stems in stem stitch, and the flower buds and the spray of mimosa in padded satin stitch. Use three strands of thread throughout.

▦ When the embroidery is completed, place it face down on a well-padded surface and press lightly, taking care not to crush the stitches.

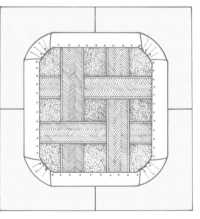

▦ Knock out the seat from the chair. Remove the hessian base and the old top cover from the seat using a ripping chisel and hammer.

▦ Mark centre of embroidery on all sides. Place the embroidery wrong side up on a flat surface. Centre the chair seat over the embroidery, making sure that the design is facing in the right direction.

▦ Pull the embroidered fabric firmly to the underside of the seat and tack in place, working from the centre of each side outwards. Tack each corner in position smoothing over the fabric to give a rounded effect.

▦ Cut a piece of hessian on the straight of grain the size of the chair seat base. Turn under the raw edges and tack in place all round the seat covering the edges of the embroidered fabric and rounding the corners.

a reminder of warm, fragrant days

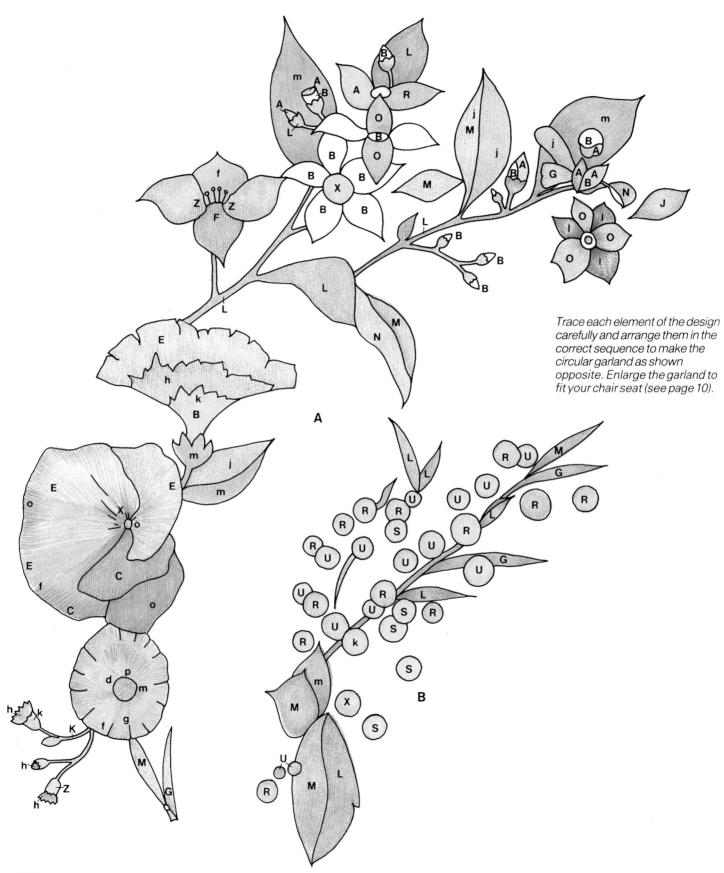

Trace each element of the design carefully and arrange them in the correct sequence to make the circular garland as shown opposite. Enlarge the garland to fit your chair seat (see page 10).

KEY

A	ecru
B	white
C	223
D	224
E	225
F	316
G	320
H	350
I	351
J	367
K	471
L	502
M	503
N	504
O	598
P	605
Q	676
R	725
S	727
T	734
U	742
V	743
W	744
X	745
Y	754
Z	778
a	739
b	818
c	819
d	828
e	912
f	927
g	928
h	945
i	951
j	3055
k	3078
l	3325
m	3347
n	3348
o	3688
p	3689
q	326

FISH FANTASY

A fine collection of fish with their asymmetrical shapes and gorgeous details has been caught and laid out for display – embroider them in hot, tropical colours for cushions as stunning as pictures. Don't labour over the close regularity of the stitches; on a white background the gaps will give the impression that the fish are painted.

MATERIALS

66cm (25in) × 48cm (18in) white cotton fabric	*Crewel needle size 6 or 7 Embroidery hoop*

Threads
DMC stranded cotton – 1 skein of each of the following:
CUSHION A: **blue** *517, 518, 519, 747;* **yellow** *704;* **pink** *956;* **pale green** *955;* **shaded green** *123*
CUSHION B: **green** *699, 702, 704;* **shaded green** *114;* **orange** *970, 972;* **yellow** *973;* **black** *310*
CUSHION C: **green** *699, 701, 890;* **blue** *797, 809;* **kingfisher** *996;* **shaded blue** *113;* **yellow** *973;* **red** *606;* **black** *310*

Embroidery Stitches
Long and short stitch, satin stitch, straight stitch.

METHOD

▦ Enlarge the design to the measurements given on the pattern (see page 10). Transfer the design to the fabric using one of the methods given on page 11 and positioning it as shown in the diagram

▦ Work with the fabric stretched in an embroidery hoop, moving the hoop as necessary.

▦ Using the close-up photograph as a stitch guide, embroider the fishes in long and short stitch and in satin stitch, and pick out the details in straight stitch. Use three strands of thread throughout.

▦ When the embroidery is completed, place it face down on a well-padded surface and press lightly, taking care not to crush the stitches.

▦ Instructions for making up the cushion covers are on page 15.

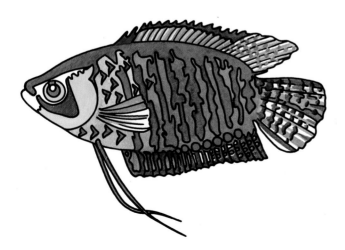

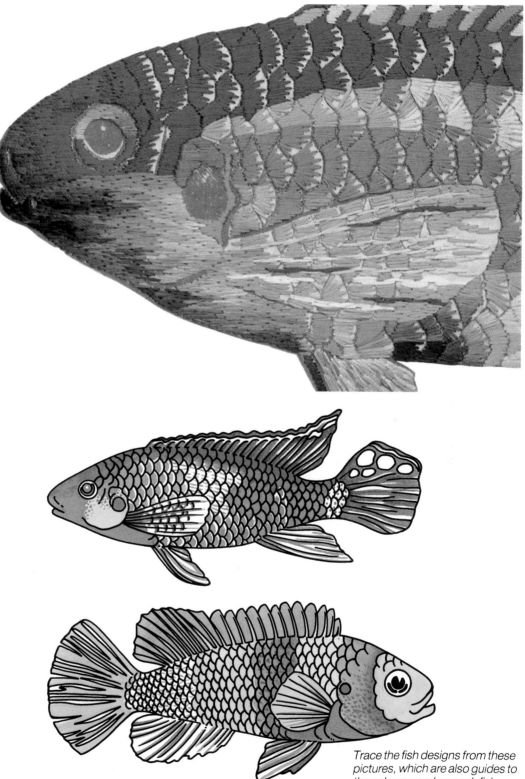

Trace the fish designs from these pictures, which are also guides to the colours used on each fish. The photograph above shows how the embroidery is worked to allow the fabric to show through.

DRAGONFLY BEDLINEN

There is no need to lie awake counting sheep when you could sleep peacefully, dreaming of dragonflies dancing over water. This very delicate set consists of a pillowcase hand embroidered with dragonfly motifs and a machine embroidered and quilted duvet cover, crossed and edged with silver piping, with a pillowcase to match. The cover is of a typically French design, with the centre left open so that the duvet can be inserted through it. If you prefer, you could fill the central square and make a conventional opening at the bottom (see page 152).

Sizes Finished duvet cover 200cm × 200cm (80in × 80in) to fit standard double duvet; pillowcases 75cm × 55cm (30in × 22in).

MATERIALS

DRAGONFLY PILLOWCASE
1.4m (1½yd) of 90cm (36in) wide white cotton piqué
2.7m (3yd) of ready-made (washable) silver piping

White sewing thread
Crewel needle size 4 or 5
Dressmakers' carbon paper
Large embroidery hoop

GEOMETRIC PILLOWCASE
1.4m (1½yd) of 90cm (36in) wide white cotton piqué
5m (5½yd) of ready-made

(washable) silver piping
White sewing thread

DUVET COVER
5.2m (5¾yd) of 90cm (36in) wide white cotton piqué
4.2m (4¾yd) of 220cm (88in) wide cotton sheeting for back and inner lining
2m (2yd) of 250cm (100in) wide

medium-weight polyester wadding
28m (30½yd) of ready-made (washable) silver piping
White sewing thread
Light coloured pencil

Threads
DRAGONFLY PILLOWCASE
*Two reels of DMC **silver** thread 281*
Anchor coton à broder size 16:

*one skein each of **grey** 398 and 399, and two skeins of **white** 1*

GEOMETRIC PILLOWCASE
*Two reels of DMC **silver** thread 281*

Embroidery stitches
Couching, padded satin stitch; these are used in the Dragonfly pillowcase. The Geometric pillowcase and the Duvet cover are both machine stitched.

METHOD

DRAGONFLY PILLOWCASE
▦ Cut a piece measuring 80cm × 60cm (32in × 24in) from the fabric.

This will be the front of the pillowcase.
▦ Trace the dragonfly design and enlarge it to the required dimensions, as shown on page 10.

▦ Using the photograph as a guide to position, transfer the design to the top left-hand corner of the fabric, using dressmakers' carbon paper and leaving a margin of 2.5cm (1in) from the raw edges.
▦ Working with the fabric stretched in the embroidery hoop, embroider the lines in couched silver thread and the dragonflies in padded satin stitch with the white thread. Embroider the spots in padded satin stitch in a random mixture of silver, white and grey, as seen in the photograph.
▦ When you have finished the embroidery, place the fabric face down on a well-padded surface and press it lightly, taking care not to crush the stitches. Trim the edges so that the finished front section measures 78cm × 58cm (31¼in × 23¼in).

FINISHING THE PILLOWCASE
▦ Cut out a rectangle of fabric 81.5cm × 58cm (32⅝in × 23¼in) for the back and another rectangle 58cm × 17.5cm (23¼in × 7in) for the flap.
▦ Turn under 5cm (2in) to the wrong side along one short edge of the back piece and then turn under 1cm (⅜in) along the raw edge to make a 4cm (1⅝in) deep hem. Stitch in place.
▦ Turn under a double 5cm (2in) hem to the wrong side along one long edge of the flap. Pin, tack and stitch in place.
▦ Pin the piping to the right side of the embroidered front. The piping should face inwards to the centre all around the edge. Stitch the piping in place 1.5cm (⅝in) from the raw edges.
▦ Assemble the pillowcase by placing the back section on top of the piped front with the right sides of the fabric facing. Align the hemmed edge of the back with the seamline on the front. Place the flap right side down over the hemmed edge of the back, matching the long raw edge of the flap with the raw edge on the front. Pin, tack and stitch, following the line of stitching for the piping.
▦ Trim and neaten the raw edges, then turn the pillowcase right side out with the flap on the inside. Press the seams.

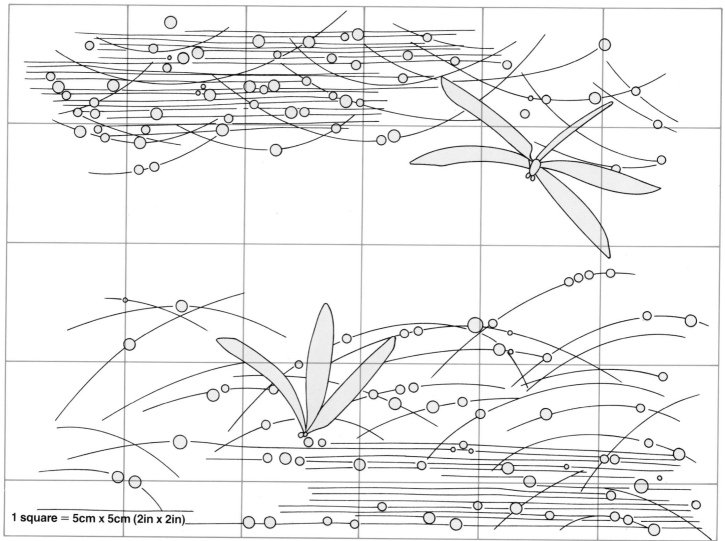

1 square = 5cm x 5cm (2in x 2in)

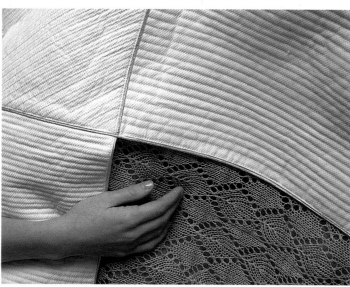

GEOMETRIC PILLOWCASE

▦ Cut a piece of cotton piqué to measure 63cm × 43cm (25¼in × 17¼in) for the centre front.

▦ With silver thread on top and white sewing cotton in the bobbin, stitch the pattern of crossing lines. Use the photograph as a guide, and position the outermost lines 12.5cm (5in) from the raw edges of the fabric.

▦ Pin the piping to the right side of the fabric. It should face inwards to the centre and should run all around the edge. Stitch the piping in place 1.5cm from the raw edges.

▦ Cut two strips of fabric measuring 58cm × 10.5cm (23¼in × 4¼in) and two strips measuring 78cm × 10.5cm

(31¼in × 4¼in). Join the strips into a frame with mitred darts, starting 1.5cm (⅝in) away from the raw inner edge and fading to nothing at the outside edge. Trim and press.

▦ Stitch the border frame to the central piece, following the stitching line of the piping and stitching the two long sides first and then the two short ones.

▦ Finish the pillowcase in the same way as the dragonfly pillowcase.

DUVET COVER

▦ Cut eight rectangles measuring 63cm × 63cm (25¼in × 25¼in) and cut the same from wadding.

▦ Using the light coloured pencil, draw the seamline around each

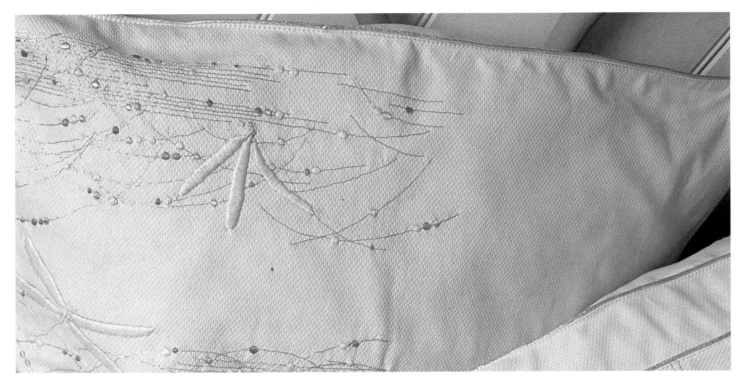

fabric piece, 1.5cm (⅝in) from the raw edge, on the right side.

▦ Back each fabric piece with a piece of wadding and tack horizontally and vertically. Using the diagram as a guide, quilt each of the squares with long machine straight stitch and white thread.

▦ Cut 63cm (25¼in) lengths of piping and stitch one each to the bottom edges of A, B and C and the top edges of F, G and H.

▦ Stitch A, D and F together to make a long strip. Trim wadding back to the seamline and trim 1cm and 5mm (⅜in and ¼in) from the seam allowances of the piping cord at each side of the seams, to layer the seam allowances. Press seams open.

▦ Join C, E and H in the same way. Stitch a length of piping, with the piping lying inwards and raw edges matching, to the inside edge of each long strip.

▦ Following the diagram, join rectangles B and G to the strips to complete the patchwork effect. Topstitch along all seams, except around the centre, close to piping.

▦ Pin piping around the outer edge, rounding the corners gently. Stitch in position.

▦ Cut four strips of piqué and four

of wadding, each measuring 203cm × 17.5cm (81¼in × 7in). Pin and tack wadding to the back of each strip, then join the strips, as for the Geometric pillowcase, to make a mitred border frame.

▦ Turn under the seam allowance around the quilted piece and topstitch it to the border, stitching just inside the piping.

▦ Cut two pieces of cotton sheeting the same size as the top. Set one piece aside and pin and stitch the other piece to the top, with right sides together and stitching around the edge of the central opening, following the seamlines of the piping. Cut out the central square from the sheeting and take to the back.

▦ Topstitch around the central opening, close to the piping.

▦ Pin piping around the outer edge, pinning through the top and the backing, with raw edges matching. Stitch in position.

▦ Take the second piece of sheeting and, with right sides of insert of duvet top and second piece of sheeting together, stitch around the outer edge, following the line of the piping, and leaving a gap for turning. Turn right side out and slipstitch to close.

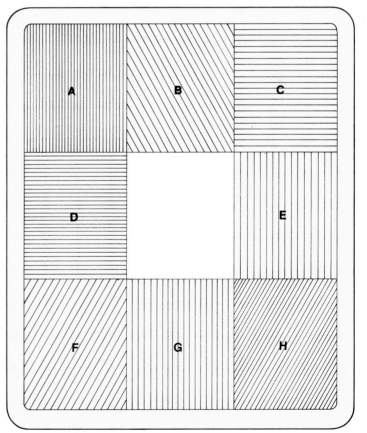

PROVENÇAL PRINTS

These flowered objects were inspired by the traditional fabrics of Provence. Use the violets to decorate a fabric-covered box, a letter file or a jewel case. The tiny swags look particularly fine on a typical abstract French print. Satin stitch and stem stitch in faded coloured silks give the fresh-washed, sun-bleached character of the original textile designs.

MATERIALS

SMALL BOX:

Flattish cardboard box with a hinged lid
Cotton fabric with a small geometric design
Crewel needle size 7 or 8
Embroidery hoop

LARGE BOX:

Cardboard box with a lid
Cotton fabric with a large floral design
Cotton fabric with a small geometric design
Crewel needle size 7 or 8
Embroidery hoop

Threads
DMC stranded cotton:
1 skein in each of the following colours:
yellow *677, 745, 746;* **green** *502, 503;* **blue** *930, 931;* **pink** *961;* **black** *310*

Threads: *DMC stranded cotton in colours to match the fabric*

Embroidery Stitches
Long and short stitch, satin stitch, stem stitch.

METHOD

FOR THE SMALL BOX:

▥ Cut a piece of geometrically patterned fabric to fit the box lid, allowing a margin of 5cm (2in) all round. Enlarge the design to fit across the lid (see page 10).

▥ Transfer the design to the fabric using one of the methods given on page 11.

▥ Work with the fabric stretched in an embroidery hoop, moving the hoop as necessary.

▥ Using the diagram as a colour guide, embroider the design in long and short stitch with two strands of thread.

FOR THE LARGE BOX:

▥ Cut a piece of the floral fabric to fit the lid, allowing a margin of 5cm (2in) all round and positioning one or two of the floral sprays attractively on the top of the lid.

▥ Work with the fabric stretched in an embroidery hoop, moving the hoop as necessary.

▥ Using the close-up photograph as a stitch guide,

embroider over the flowers and leaves: use long and short stitch for the petals and leaves, pick out tiny areas of colour in satin stitch and work the stems and outlines in stem stitch. Use two strands of thread in matching colours throughout.

TO MAKE UP THE BOXES:

▥ Place the embroidery face down on a well-padded surface and press lightly, taking care not to crush the stitches.

▥ Trim the margins to 2cm (¾in) and follow the instructions shown in the diagrams for covering the boxes.

Trace pattern for the small box.

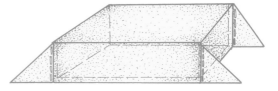

Place the fabric over the box with wrong sides outside. Pin out excess fabric equally at each corner in line with box corners. Remove fabric and stitch each corner level with box edge. Trim off excess fabric and press seam open. Replace over box and stick in place. Fold excess fabric to inside and stick.

VENETIAN ELEGANCE

Luxuriously elegant cushion covers and a table centrepiece to match make a light-hearted tribute to the great Italian architect of the sixteenth century, Andrea Palladio, who described the classical colonnades which often extended from his villas as 'arms to receive those who come near the house'. These sophisticated embroideries with their gentle, muted tones would blend perfectly with a neutral, modern setting, or with rag-rubbed or marbled walls.

Sizes The cushion covers measure 47cm × 47cm (18½in × 18½in); centrepiece 50cm × 50cm (20in × 20in).

MATERIALS

FOR EACH CUSHION COVER

40cm × 40cm (16in × 16in) of white linen or cotton fabric	Crewel needle size 5 or 6
Two 50cm × 50cm (20in × 20in) squares of dark fawn linen or cotton fabric	Dressmakers' carbon paper in a dark colour
Matching sewing thread	Ruler and chalk marking pencil
	Large embroidery hoop

CENTREPIECE

52cm × 52cm (20¾in × 20¾in) of white linen or cotton fabric	Crewel needle size 5 or 6
Matching sewing thread	Dressmakers' carbon paper
	Large embroidery hoop

Threads

VILLA CAPRA ROTONDA
DMC stranded cotton: one skein each of **shaded brown** 105, **brown** 433, **beige** 3046 and 3047, **grey** 535, 642 and 644, and **ecru**

VILLA GODI
DMC stranded cotton: one skein each of **shaded brown** 105, **brown** 433, **grey** 415, 535 and 646, **blue grey** 927, and **ecru**, and two skeins of **grey** 3072

VILLA PIOVENE
DMC stranded cotton: one skein each of **shaded brown** 105, **brown** 407, **grey** 535, **peach** 950, and **ecru**, and two skeins of **peach** 948

CENTREPIECE
DMC stranded cotton: one skein each of **grey** 3072, **blue grey** 926, **blue** 930, **peach** 948, **beige** 950, and **fawn** 3046; two skeins of **fawn** 3047, and four skeins of **dark grey** 535

Embroidery stitches

CUSHION COVERS
Satin stitch for the solid areas and back stitch for the lettering and borders.

CENTREPIECE
Satin stitch and cross stitch for the solid areas and back stitch for the outlines and lettering.

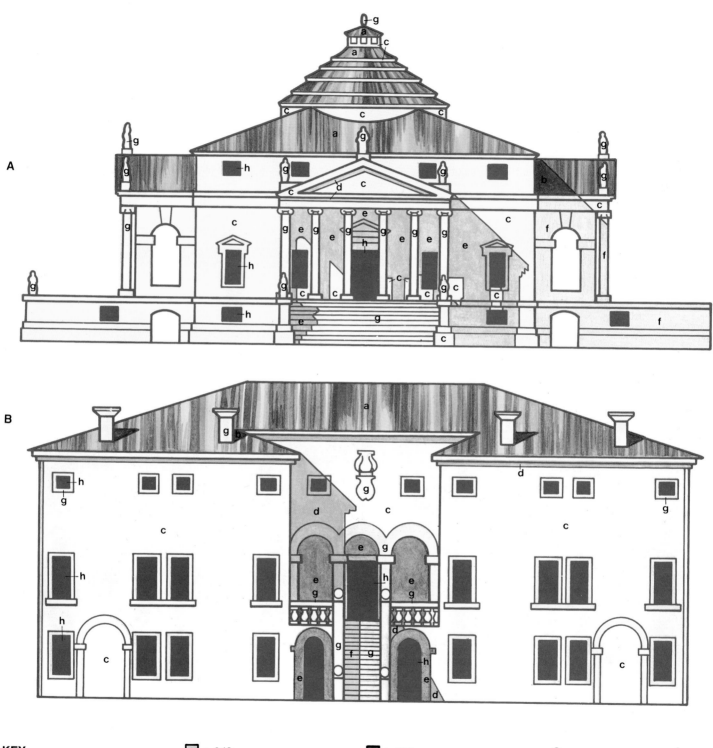

A

B

KEY
A

a *105*
b *433*
c *3047*
d *3046*

e *642*
f *644*
g *ecru*
h *535 also* **B** *and* **C**

B

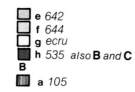

a *105*

b *433*
c *3072*
d *927*
e *646*
f *415*
g *ecru*

C

a *105*
b *948*
c *950*
d *407*
e *ecru*

c

METHOD

CUSHION COVER

▦ Each cushion cover is made in the same way. Start by tracing the chosen design and enlarging it to the required dimensions, as shown on page 10.

▦ Transfer the design to the centre of the white fabric using dressmakers' carbon paper. Draw in the border with the chalk pencil and ruler, approximately 5cm (2in) in from the raw edges of the fabric, following the grainlines.

▦ Using the photograph and diagram as stitch guides, embroider the solid areas of the design in satin stitch. Work the border and the appropriate lettering in back stitch using the grey thread, 535. Work with the fabric stretched in the embroidery hoop and use three strands of thread throughout.

▦ When the embroidery is completed, place the fabric face down on a well-padded surface and press it lightly, taking care not to crush the stitches.

FINISHING THE COVER

▦ On one piece of fawn fabric, cut out a central opening measuring 35cm (14in) square to accommodate the embroidered square. Turn under 1.5cm (⅝in) to the wrong side all around the opening, taking care to snip into the corners so that the fabric will lie flat. Tack the turning in place.

▦ Position the fabric over the embroidery so that the embroidery shows evenly through the opening, then pin and tack the layers together. Machine stitch

through the fabric neatly round the opening 2mm (⅛in) from edge.

▦ Pin the front and back pieces of the cushion cover together with right sides facing and machine stitch them together round the edge, leaving an opening along one side and taking a 1.5cm (⅝in) seam allowance.

▦ Snip across the corners, press the seam and turn the cover to the right side.

▦ Insert the cushion pad and slipstitch neatly along the opening to close the cover.

ANDREA PALLADIO   1508-1580

VILLA CAPRA ROTONDA

VILLA GODI   VILLA PIOVENE

VILLA ROTONDA

A

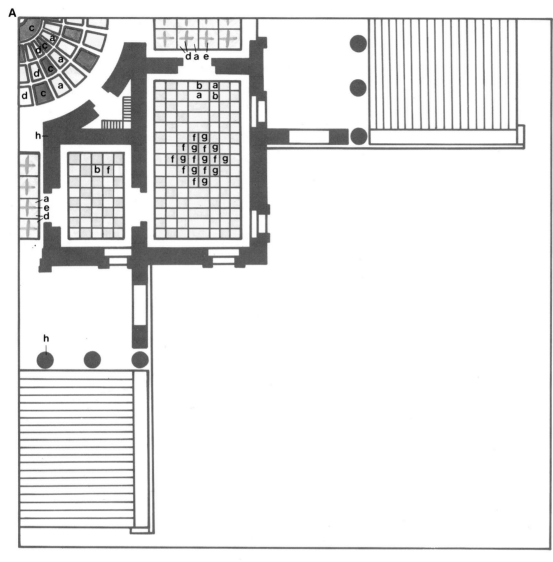

CENTREPIECE

▦ Start by making the border and neatening the edges of the cloth. Turn under and press a 1cm (⅜in) single hem all around the fabric square, mitring the corners neatly. Work a border of close machine zigzag stitch (or satin stitch by hand), covering the raw edges and making the hem.

▦ Between 6.5cm and 8cm (3½in and 4in) in from the edge of the cloth, make three narrow lines of satin stitch, set close together and running from edge to edge down each side, crossing at the corners.

THE EMBROIDERY

▦ One quarter of the design is shown, with A being the centre point. Trace the complete design and enlarge it to the required dimensions following the instructions given on page 10.

▦ Transfer the design to the centre of the cloth using the carbon paper method given on page 11.

▦ Using the photograph as a stitch guide, embroider the solid portions of the design in satin stitch and overstitch them with cross stitch where this is indicated on the design. Work the outlines and lettering in back stitch. Work with the fabric stretched in the embroidery hoop and use the three strands of thread throughout.

▦ When the embroidery is finished, place the cloth face down on a well-padded surface and press it lightly, taking care not to crush the stitches.

KEY

▢ **a**	*3047*
▢ **b**	*948*
▤ **c**	*930*
▢ **d**	*3072*
▤ **e**	*926*
▢ **f**	*950*
▢ **g**	*3046*
▣ **h**	*535*

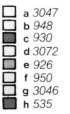

BUTTERFLY PICNIC

A host of butterflies with dazzling wings dances around a damask tablecloth, spilling over onto the napkins – what better setting could you provide for an elegant outdoor feast on a summer's day? Perhaps a few real butterflies will be lured into joining you if you are really lucky. The damask background provides a subtle extra dimension against which you can display as many or as few butterflies as you wish, depending on your personal taste and how energetic you are feeling.

Size: tablecloth 115cm×135cm (45in×54in); napkin 40cm×40cm (16in×16in). The quanties given are for the tablecloth in the photograph but you can easily make yours smaller or larger.

MATERIALS

2m (2¼yd) of 140cm (56in) wide cotton or linen damask – sufficient for one tablecloth and up to six napkins
DMC stranded cotton, one skein each of the following colours: brown 300 and 976, black 310, grey 413, yellow 444, 676 and 742, orange 972 and 973, blue 792, 799 and 800, turquoise 995 and 996, lilac 553, green 701, 907, 943, 991 and 993, and white
14m (15½yd) of 13mm (½in) wide blue satin bias binding (for tablecloth and six napkins)
Crewel needle size 6 or 7
Tracing paper
Dressmakers' carbon paper
Matching sewing thread
Note If the above yarn is unobtainable, refer to page 191.

METHOD

▦ Using a pencil mark one rectangle 115cm×135cm (45in×54in) for the tablecloth and six 40cm (16in) squares for the napkins on the damask. Cut out, allowing a small margin of spare fabric around each for fraying.
▦ Enlarge the butterfly motifs onto tracing paper and transfer them to the cloth, using the photograph as a general guide to positioning, but choosing for yourself how many motifs you wish to repeat and where.
▦ Using three strands of thread throughout and keeping the fabric stretched in the embroidery hoop, embroider the motifs. Embroider the butterflies in satin stitch, using the photograph as a stitch guide.
▦ For each napkin, work one or two butterflies in one corner.
▦ When the embroidered pieces are completed, place them face downwards on a well-padded surface and press them lightly.
▦ Trim all pieces back to the marked pencil line. For each napkin, take a 165cm (66in)

length of binding. Turn 6mm (¼in) under at one short end and with the binding out flat and matching the folded end to the edge at one side of the napkin, lay the binding along one side, with the edge of the binding a scant 6mm (¼in) in from the raw edge of the napkin. Pin and tack. At the corner adjust the binding so that it will run easily around the corner when brought over to cover the edge. Work round the napkin in this manner. At the final corner, turn under the short raw edge of the binding for 6mm (¼in), folding it at a mitred angle and trimming away any spare length. Make sure that it will completely cover the other end.
▦ Stitch the binding to napkin, bring it over to the wrong side, making mitred folds at the corners, and pin and slipstitch by hand to the other side. (For a more hand-finished effect, machine the binding to the wrong side first and then slipstitch to the right side.) Make a few concealed stitches at the corners to hold.
▦ Complete the tablecloth in the same manner.

EASTER TABLECLOTH

Breakfast on Easter morning is a family ritual in France as elsewhere, complete with brightly coloured eggs, Easter bunnies, lambs and all the other images of springtime and renewal. Here is a tablecloth in the full Easter tradition, dotted with bells, flowers, rabbits seriously engaged in transporting their loads of eggs and hens apparently unperturbed by their multicoloured produce. Children will enjoy it openly and adults secretly, and you will inevitably find yourself using it not just for Easter day but for birthday parties and a host of special occasions. These cheerful little designs are immensely versatile and could be used to decorate many other items for children, including pillowcases, pyjamas, T-shirts, bags, or even the hem of a nursery curtain.

Size 124cm × 124cm (49½in × 49½in).

MATERIALS

130cm × 130cm (52in × 52in) of fine white cotton fabric
4.2m (4¾yd) of 1cm (⅜in) wide yellow ribbon

Yellow and white sewing threads
Crewel needle size 5 or 6
Dressmakers' carbon paper
Large embroidery hoop

Threads

DMC stranded cotton: one skein of **yellow** 742 for the chicks; one skein of **blue** 995 for the ribbons; one skein of **brown** 921 for the rabbits; oddments of stranded cotton in various shades of **green, blue, orange, yellow, beige, ecru, red, pink, mauve, grey, brown** and **black**

Embroidery stitches

Satin stitch, long and short stitch, straight stitch, back stitch and stem stitch.

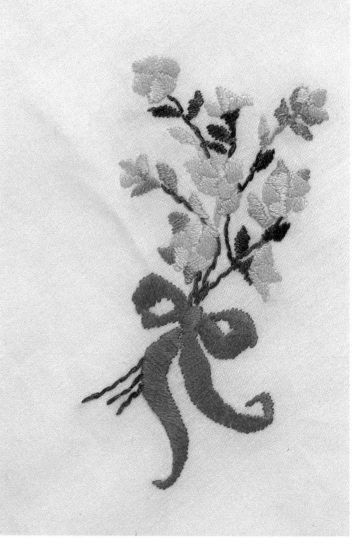

134

METHOD

▦ The two motifs shown above and those on page 134 are all shown full size. All other motifs are shown two-thirds full size.

▦ Trace all motifs, then take the small size ones and enlarge them to full size as described on page 10 (in this case the small grid should have 1cm/³⁄₈in squares and the full-size grid should have 1.5cm/⁵⁄₈in squares). It may be easier simply to trace over the main outlines of the more complicated motifs and fill in the minor details by hand afterwards. Using the photograph as a guide to position, transfer the motifs to the fabric by the carbon paper method.

▦ Work with the fabric stretched in the embroidery hoop and re-position it as necessary. Embroider the motifs mainly in satin stitch and long and short stitch, picking out the details in stem stitch, back stitch and straight stitch. Use the close-up photographs as stitch and colour blending guides and work with three strands of thread throughout.

▦ When the embroidery is completed, place the fabric face down on a well-padded surface and press it lightly, taking care not to crush the stitches.

FINISHING

▦ Turn under a double 1.5cm hem along all edges of the fabric, mitring the corners (see page 14). Pin and hem by hand.

▦ Cut the ribbon into four strips of equal length. Join the strips into a square, placing them right sides together and stitching the ends at a 45 degree angle to make mitred corners. Trim and press. Pin the ribbon square in place on the tablecloth, making sure that it is positioned an equal distance from the edge on all sides.

▦ Sew the ribbon to the tablecloth by machine, using either a close zigzag stitch or a small running stitch, and keeping close to each edge of the ribbon. Stitch each edge in the same direction, to avoid ruckles.

137

COUNTRYSIDE DREAMS

Delicate wild roses transform white linen or cotton sheeting into luxurious bedding. One spray looks romantic – several scattered across the fabric cover are a display of consummate skill. The rambling motif looks just as fitting stitched on long curtains of lawn or cotton, which filter the light.

MATERIALS

White cotton sheet, either single- or double-bed size.	Crewel needle size 7 or 8 Embroidery hoop

Threads
Anchor stranded cotton in the following colours: **red** 22, 334; **pink** 49, 52, 57; **yellow** 293; **gold** 306, 307; **green** 213, 214, 216, 256, 258, 267, 855; **brown** 905; **beige** 378; **cream** 386; **black** 403; **white** 1.

Embroidery Stitches
Stem stitch, padded satin stitch, satin stitch, straight stitch, darning stitch.

METHOD

▤ Enlarge the design to four times the size of the photograph pattern (see page 10). Transfer the design to the sheet using the pricking and pouncing method given on page 11.

▤ Work with the fabric stretched in an embroidery hoop, moving the hoop as necessary.

▤ Use the photographs as colour guides and work with two strands of thread.

▤ Embroider the leaves, stems and rosebuds in closely worked rows of stem stitch to fill each shape.

▤ Embroider the rosehips in padded satin stitch using two shades of red. Work the centres of the roses in satin stitch and pick out the details in straight stitch.

▤ Embroider the rose petals in parallel rows of darning stitch – each stitch should be about 5mm (¼in) long and pick up only one or two threads of fabric.

▤ Work the larger thorns in stem stitch, the smaller ones in straight stitch.

▤ When the embroidery is completed, place it face down on a well-padded surface and press lightly, taking care not to crush the stitches.

Embroider a section of the spray on a pillowcase to complement the bedcover. Place the motif at the side of the pillowcase, rather than in the centre, to avoid sleeping on the embroidery.

Trace off the design and enlarge it (see page 10) so that it is approximately four times larger than the tracing. Transfer it to the sheet using the pricking and pouncing method given on page 11. Use the photograph as a guide to the stitching and the colours. When working the rose petals, keep the stitches of equal size.

CULINARY ALLUSIONS

Whether your cuisine is enriched with fresh herbs snipped from your garden or a savoury mixture of seafoods, these attractive aprons should help to make cooking a pleasure rather than a chore. The marine collection is embroidered entirely in stem stitch against a blue background, while the chives and parsley, complete with realistic-looking scissors and string, are embroidered in a variety of stitches. Both aprons are made to the same basic pattern, though the herbal version has patch pockets.

Size 80cm × 80cm (32in × 32in).

MATERIALS

SEAFOOD APRON
*1m (1yd) of 90cm (36in) wide blue
    cotton fabric
Matching sewing thread
2.9m (3yd) of 2cm (¾in) wide
    matching blue tape*

*Dressmakers' pattern paper
Dressmakers' carbon paper in a
    light colour
Crewel needle size 3 or 4
Large embroidery hoop*

HERB APRON
*1.1m (1¼yd) of 90cm (36in) wide
    white cotton fabric
Matching sewing thread
2.9m (3yd) of 2cm (¾in) wide
    white tape
Dressmakers' pattern paper*

*Dressmakers' carbon paper
Dressmakers' chalk pencil
Crewel needles size 6 and 7
Large chenille needle
Large embroidery hoop*

Threads
SEAFOOD APRON
*DMC stranded cotton: four
    skeins of **white***

HERB APRON
*DMC stranded cotton: one skein
    each of **ecru, beige** 640 and
    3047, **grey** 318, 414, 415 and*

*762, and two skeins each of
    green 122 and 988*

Embroidery stitches
SEAFOOD APRON
Stem stitch

HERB APRON
Stem stitch, straight stitch, long and short stitch and Chinese knots.

METHOD

MAKING THE APRON
▦ Scale up the diagram onto dressmakers' pattern paper and cut out. For the seafood apron, cut out the main piece and a matching pair of facings; for the herb apron, cut out the main piece, a pair of facings and two patch pockets.
▦ Taking a 1cm (⅜in) seam

allowance and with right sides together, stitch a facing to each side of the apron, from neck edge to side edge. Holding facings out flat, narrow hem all other edges of the apron, including short edges of facings. Turn under and press a 1cm (⅜in) seam along remaining long edge of each facing. Bring the facings to the back of the apron and press.

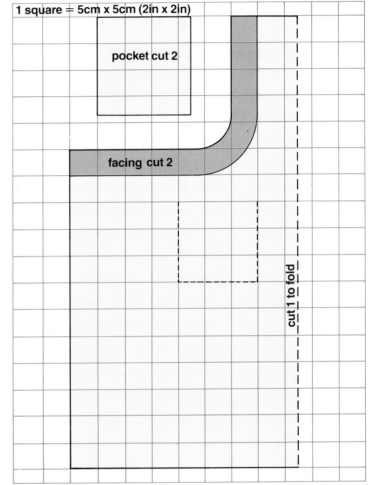

1 square = 5cm x 5cm (2in x 2in)

pocket cut 2

facing cut 2

cut 1 to fold

■ Topstitch facings to apron, close to both pressed edges, leaving a channel for the tape.

■ Cut the tape into two equal lengths and thread through the channels. Adjust to leave an adequate length for ties at neck and back, then stitch across at neck edge and side to hold ties in position.

■ For herb apron, turn under 1cm (⅜in) and then 2.5cm (1in) along the top edge of each pocket section and stitch. Press under a double hem of 1cm (⅜in) on all other sides of each pocket and topstitch in place on apron.

SEAFOOD EMBROIDERY

■ Trace the fish and shell design and enlarge it to the dimensions given, as shown on page 10.

■ Following the photograph as a guide to position, transfer the individual motifs to the apron, using dressmakers' carbon paper.

■ Working with the apron stretched in an embroidery hoop, embroider the motifs in stem stitch, using the stranded cotton double in the needle.

■ When the embroidery is finished, place the apron face down on a well-padded surface and press it lightly, taking care not to crush the stitches.

HERB EMBROIDERY

■ Scale up the chive and parsley motifs and, using the photograph as a guide to position, transfer them to the apron with dressmakers' carbon paper.

■ Slip a pair of scissors into the other pocket and draw around the outline of the handles, using the dressmakers' chalk pencil. On the front of the same pocket, draw a line to represent the piece of string.

■ Working with the apron stretched in an embroidery hoop, embroider the motifs as follows: the chives and parsley stems are worked in stem stitch, using two strands of green and the size 7 crewel needle.

■ The bobbles on the parsley are formed by Chinese knots worked with six strands of green 988 and 12 strands of green 122 together in the chenille needle. They are linked to the parsley stems with

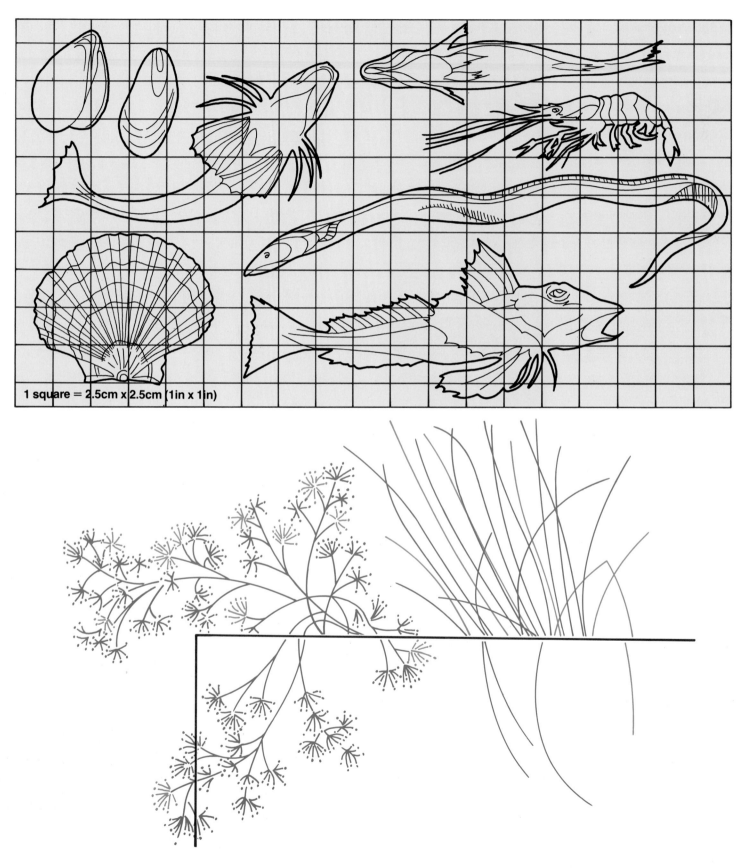

1 square = 2.5cm x 2.5cm (1in x 1in)

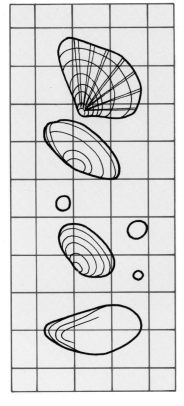

straight stitches, worked with two strands of the same green as the relevant stem and using the size 7 needle.

▦ Embroider the string in stem stitch, using six strands each of ecru, beige 640 and beige 3047 together in the chenille needle.

▦ The scissors are embroidered in long and short stitch in the four shades of grey. Use three strands of thread in the size 6 crewel needle and blend the colours from light to dark to achieve the effect of light shining at an angle on the scissors.

LEMON AND LIME SQUARES

Cross stitch is easy to follow and satisfyingly simple to do well, but you need not limit yourself to squared canvas if you enjoy this embroidery. The lemons and leaves are stitched through canvas which provides an easy-to-use grid on a fine-weave white, ready-made tablecloth. The lime and leaf-green cross-stitched overcloth is made by joining embroidered squares with herringbone stitches. There's a variety of designs, offering you all kinds of different settings.

MATERIALS FOR TABLECLOTH

Ready-made white cotton or linen tablecloth, approximately 1.8m (6ft) × 2m (6ft 6in)	8 pieces of single-thread 12-gauge canvas, each 15cm (6in) × 18cm (7in) Crewel needle size 5 or 6

Threads
DMC stranded cotton in the following colours:
6 skeins of **green** 701, 895; 5 skeins of **yellow** 445; 4 skeins of **yellow** 444, 972; 3 skeins of **green** 987; 3 skeins of **cream** 746

Embroidery Stitch
Cross stitch: each square on the chart represents one cross stitch worked over one vertical and one horizontal canvas thread.

METHOD FOR TABLECLOTH

▦ Each piece of canvas is slightly larger than the lemon motif, providing a regular grid on which to work the cross-stitch lemons.
▦ Tack the rectangles of canvas to the tablecloth, positioning them as shown in the photograph with two lemon motifs at each corner of the cloth.
▦ Embroider the design carefully following the chart. Stitch through both the canvas and the base cloth, using six strands of thread.
▦ When the embroidery is completed, carefully cut away the surplus canvas close to the stitching. Gently pull the remaining canvas threads from beneath the stitching with a pair of tweezers; avoid snagging.
▦ Place the cloth face down on a well-padded surface and press lightly, taking care not to crush the stitches.

Place the motifs at each corner.

MATERIALS FOR OVERCLOTH

6 squares of white Hardanger-
type 12-gauge fabric, each
35cm (14in) × 35cm (14in)

Crewel needle size 7 or 8
Crewel needle size 4 or 5
White sewing thread

Threads
DMC stranded cotton: 4 skeins of
each of the following colours:
design 1 **green** 989, 3348;
design 2 **green** 580, 909; design
3 **green** 3348, **kingfisher blue**
996; design 4 **green** 986, 988;
design 5 **green** 701, 704; design
6 **green** 701, 895; plus 4 skeins
of **green** 701 for joining the
squares

Embroidery Stitches
Cross stitch for working the
designs: one square on the chart
represents one cross stitch
worked over one woven block of
the fabric; feather stitch for joining
the squares.

METHOD FOR OVERCLOTH

▦ Run a vertical and a horizontal
line of tacking through the centre
of each square of fabric to
correspond with the centre lines
on the charts.
▦ Embroider the designs from
the charts, working from the
centre outwards. Use three
strands of thread and the finer
crewel needle throughout.
▦ Repeat the patterns on the
charts until each area of
embroidery measures 30cm
(12in) × 30cm (12in).

▦ Turn a double 1cm (⅜in) hem
all round each square (see page
14 for instructions for mitring the
corners) and hand stitch with
white thread.
▦ When the squares are
completed, place them face
down on a well-padded surface
and press lightly, taking care not
to crush the stitches.
▦ Join the squares edge to
edge, as shown in the diagram,
by working a row of feather stitch
with six strands of green 701
thread and the larger crewel
needle. Press the joins lightly.

● 701   ● 704

*The overcloth is made up of these
six different cross-stitch squares.*

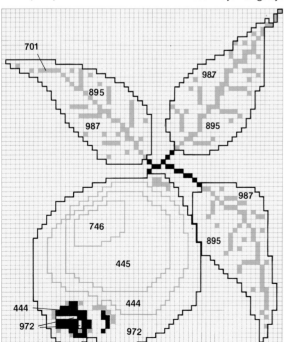

● 986   ● 988

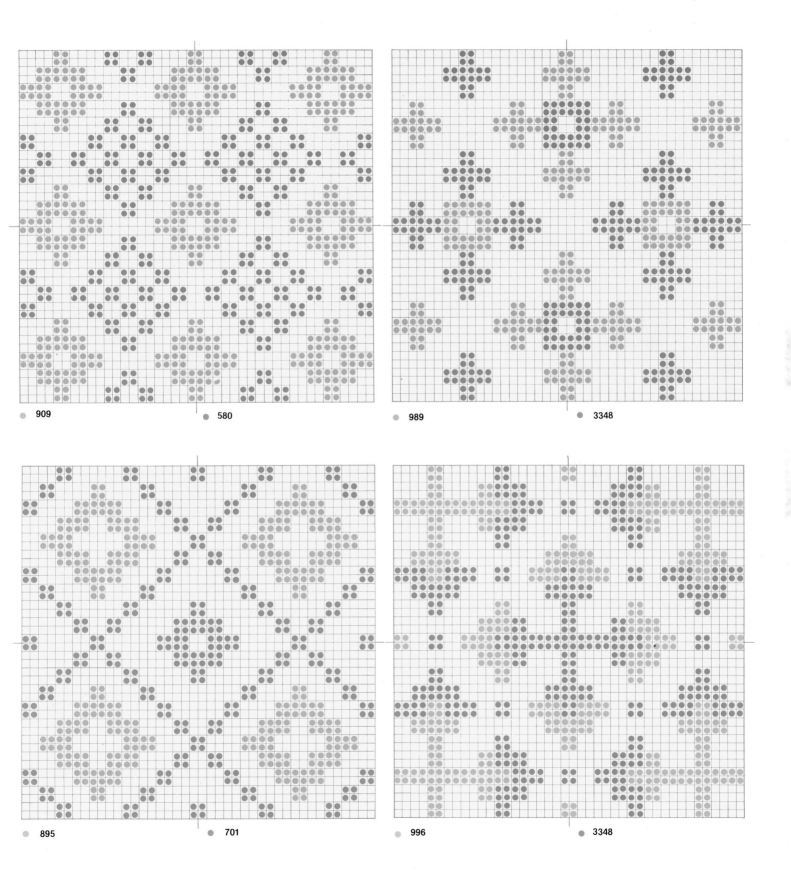

909   580

989   3348

895   701

996   3348

BOUND WITH BOWS

An attractive tablemat and matching napkin help to set the scene for a celebration, giving your table an appropriately light and festive air, whatever the occasion. Choose bright red or green for Christmas or pretty pastels for a summer tea party; pick a contrast fabric which will tone with your curtains or other elements of your decor, or make a harlequin set with a different colour for every member of the family.

Sizes: tablemat approximately 49cm×29cm (19½in×11½in); napkin 38cm (15¼in) square.

MATERIALS

Quantities are for one mat and one napkin:	Bonding fabric
50cm (⅝yd) of 90cm (36in) wide plain white cotton	Tracing paper
20cm (8in) of 90cm (36in) wide contrast fabric	Dressmakers' pattern paper
	Matching embroidery cotton
	Matching thread

METHOD

FOR THE TABLEMAT

▦ Cut a piece of squared paper 50cm×40cm (20in×16in). Fold it carefully in half both ways (into four) and press folds. Draw up the diagram onto one side of the folded paper, with the straight edges running along the folded paper edges. Keeping the paper folded, cut along the shaped outer edge. Unfold the pattern.

▦ Using the pattern, cut out one placemat from white cotton – a seam allowance of 6mm (¼in) all around is included.

▦ Now draw in the border on the pattern, making it 3.5cm (1½in) wide all around (this includes seam allowances). Using tracing paper, make patterns for the border – one for the sides and one for the top and bottom, angling the corners so that the strips will join at a mitred angle and adding 6mm (¼in) seam allowances at either end.

▦ Cut two sides and two top/bottom strips from contrast fabric and join to make a continuous border frame. Turn in and tack a 6mm (¼in) allowance around the inner edge, clipping up to the fold where necessary.

▦ With right side of border to wrong side of mat, pin, tack and stitch border to mat, taking a 6mm (¼in) seam allowance all around. Taking notches out of seam allowance where necessary, bring border to right side of mat. Topstitch by machine or blanket stitch by hand to hold border in place around inner edge.

▦ Scale up and trace off bow pattern, once with and once without ribbon ends. Mark both shapes on bonding fabric and cut out roughly, allowing a little extra all around. Iron bonding to wrong side of contrast fabric and cut out both shapes.

▦ Pull back from bow with ends and position at top right corner of mat. Iron in place, then blanket stitch around the outer edge and the knot, anchoring the bow. Add crease lines in stem stitch and scattered dots in satin stitch.

▦ Remove backing from bow without ends and iron to wrong side of contrast fabric, then cut out. Blanket stitch around inner lines and knot of contrast bow, adding crease lines in stem stitch as before. Position prepared bow upside down at left-hand corner. Blanket stitch in place, sewing all around the outer edge but only attaching the bow to the mat at either end, leaving the central portion free, to hold the napkin.

FOR THE NAPKIN

▦ Cut out one piece of white cotton 38cm (15¼in) square. Bind the napkin in the same way as the placemat, but cutting strips 2.2cm (⅞in) wide, to make a finished border 1cm (⅜in) wide.

▦ Trace a bow shape and cut from contrast fabric. Iron to bonding fabric, remove backing, and then iron and blanket stitch to napkin, adding stem stitch and satin stitch details as before.

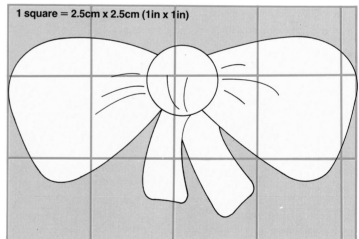

1 square = 2.5cm x 2.5cm (1in x 1in)

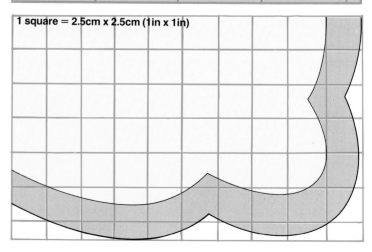

1 square = 2.5cm x 2.5cm (1in x 1in)

HUNGARIAN DUVET COVER

Hungarian folk art captures the profusion and rich colours of tender wild flowers in vivid embroideries that hum with life like a gypsy dance. Here, a collection of the flower motifs that are traditionally used to decorate Magyar blouses are entwined to make a deeper inner border for a glowing duvet cover. The result is splendid, but the cover is not as complicated to embroider as it might appear: the stitches used are basically very simple and the lavish effect comes from the well-planned use of colours.

Size Finished cover measures 136cm × 200cm (54in × 80in), to fit standard single-bed duvet.

MATERIALS

4.2m (4¾yd) of 140cm (56in) wide white cotton sheeting fabric
White sewing thread
1m (1yd) of nylon press stud tape

Dressmakers' carbon paper in a dark colour
Crewel needle size 3 or 4
Large embroidery hoop

Threads

*DMC pearl cotton No. 5: three skeins each of **pink** 335 and 818, **shaded pink** 48, **green** 581, 895 and 993, **shaded green** 92, 101 and 122, **white, shaded brown** 105, and **shaded turquoise** 91, and four skeins each of **red***

*666 and 814, **shaded red** 57, 99, 107 and 115, **orange** 900, 817 and 947, **shaded orange** 51, **yellow** 402, 973, and 977, **shaded yellow** 108 and 111, and **shaded blue** 67, 93 and 121*

Embroidery stitches

Satin stitch and stem stitch

METHOD

THE EMBROIDERY

▦ First cut the fabric into two equal rectangles and set one aside for the underneath of the cover.

▦ Trace the three sections of the garland design and join them carefully into one continuous strip. Enlarge the design to the required dimensions, as shown on page 10, again using tracing paper so that you can reverse it.

▦ Using the diagram as a guide to position, transfer the garland sections to the fabric.

▦ Working with the fabric stretched in the embroidery hoop, embroider the flowers and foliage in satin stitch and the stems in stem stitch.

▦ When the embroidery is completed, place the fabric face down on a well-padded surface and press it lightly, taking care not to crush the stitches.

FINISHING THE COVER

▦ Fold under and stitch a double 2.5cm (1in) hem along the bottom edge of both pieces of fabric.

▦ Place the two pieces of fabric together, with right sides facing, aligning the hemmed edges. Sewing along the hemline, machine stitch the two pieces together for 25cm (10in) from each side, leaving a central opening.

▦ Trim the press stud tape to measure 3cm (1¼in) longer than the opening. Position the two strips of tape along the edges of the opening so that they will match when the cover is turned right side out. Stitch along the top and bottom edges of each strip, sewing through the hemmed edge only. Stitch the hems together at each side of the opening, enclosing the raw ends of the tape.

▦ Fold the cover with wrong sides facing and make a French seam around the remaining three sides: pin and stitch 1cm (⅜in) from the edge along all three sides and trim back to 6mm (¼in). Turn the cover wrong side out and stitch along all three sides again, 1cm (⅜in) from the edge, enclosing the raw edges and completing the seam.

▦ Turn the finished cover right side out and press the seams.

1 *Enlarge to make joined garland
74cm (20½in)*

2

3

It will help you to transfer the design if you first rule a base line on the fabric, using tailor's chalk. The line should be 74cm (20½in) long and positioned 60cm (24in) up from the bottom edge of the fabric, an equal distance in from the sides. Using a set square, rule lines running upwards from each end of the base line, to act as guidelines for the side edges of the garland. The garland runs from **A** (left) to **B** (right) along the bottom line. The sides start with **C** at the bottom left and **A** at the bottom right, and finish with **B** at the top. The trace pattern is then turned over and repeated at the top, wrong side uppermost, to run from **B** at the top left to **A** at the top right, flower **A** being repeated at the top left to fill the gap between the two pattern repeats. When stitching the design, blend the colours to achieve a natural effect, varying them as indicated. For the flowers marked **1, 2, 3, 4, 5, 7** and **8**, use colours 115, 48, 57, 335, 107, 666, 818, 814, 900 and 99; flowers marked **6** and **10** are embroidered in colours 973, 977, 108, 402, 111, 817, 947, 51 and 105, and flowers marked **2** and **5** can also be stitched in these colours; for **11** and **12** use 67, 91, 93, 121 and white; and for **9** (stalks and leaves) use 92, 101, 122, 581, 895 and 993.

FALL OF LEAVES

A delicate shadow-work tablecloth of fine organdie, with napkins to match, captures the autumnal splendour of a French forest of sweet chestnut trees at that transitional time of year when the leaves begin to drift earthwards and the nuts ripen to form a delicious harvest to savour through the winter. In this embroidery technique, worked here with the traditional closed herringbone stitch, the threads are carried across the reverse side of a semi-transparent fabric. As shown below, the stitches can be worked from either side of the fabric, and they are used here to convey the impression of sunlight filtering through branches.

Size The tablecloth measures 107cm × 192cm (42in × 77in); each napkin measures 40cm × 40cm (16in × 16in).

MATERIALS

115cm (45in) wide fine cotton organdie as follows: 2m (2¼yd) for the cloth 44cm × 44cm (17½in × 17½in) for each napkin	Matching sewing thread Crewel needle size 8 or 9 HB lead pencil Large embroidery hoop

Threads

DMC stranded cotton: one skein each of **brown** 355, 632, 780, **rust** 922 and 976, **gold** 729, and **green** 469, 470, 3051 and 3348

Embroidery stitches

Closed herringbone stitch worked on the reverse of the fabric

METHOD

▦ Trace the leaf design and enlarge it to the required dimensions, as shown on page 10.

▦ Using the photograph as a guide to position, transfer the design to the fabric by placing the design under the fabric and tracing it through with the HB pencil. The pencil lines should be on the wrong side of the fabric.

▦ Work with the fabric stretched in the embroidery hoop and reposition it as necessary. With fine fabric of this type it is best to bind your embroidery hoop to help to prevent any possible damage. Take a length of bias binding tape and wrap it firmly round the inner ring of the hoop until all the wood is covered. Secure the ends with masking tape. As a further precaution, and to prevent the fabric from moving in the hoop, place a sheet of tissue paper over the fabric before fitting it in the hoop, then tear away the centre, revealing the area to be embroidered.

▦ Embroider the leaves on the reverse of the fabric in closed herringbone stitch, using two strands of thread in the needle throughout.

Closed herringbone stitch right side

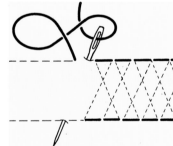

wrong side

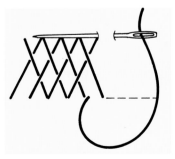

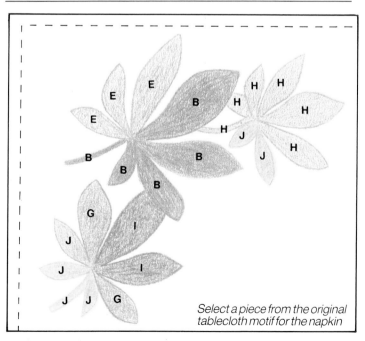

Select a piece from the original tablecloth motif for the napkin

When the embroidery is finished, place the fabric face down on a well-padded surface and press it lightly, taking care not to crush the stitches.

 Turn under a double 2cm (¾in) hem all around the fabric and hem by hand or machine.

 For the napkin, stitch the embroidery in the same way as for the cloth, but use the small leaf design. To finish the napkin, turn under a double 1cm (⅜in) hem and finish as for the cloth.

KEY

A	*355*
B	*632*
C	*780*
D	*922*
E	*976*
F	*729*
G	*469*
H	*470*
I	*3051*
J	*3348*

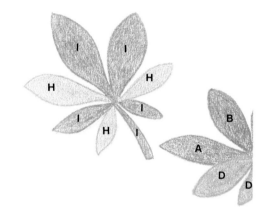

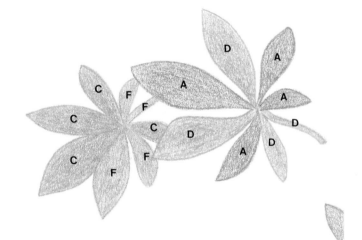

Enlarge 3 times

CELEBRATION TIME

Clouds of net, as light and airy as champagne bubbles and decorated with feathers, ribbons and tiny balls, create a magical party scene for Christmas, a birthday, an engagement, a wedding anniversary or whatever you choose. If you are too inhibited even to dine by candlelight, this is not for you, but if you share the Gallic love for the dramatic and for creating a romantic or festive atmosphere, then you will appreciate this instant transformation.

Sizes: to fit your own requirements.

MATERIALS

FOR THE DOOR CURTAIN

Net fabric – see below for
  quantity
Small amounts of plain cotton
  fabric for appliqué
Chenille braid

2cm (¾in) diameter polystyrene
  balls
Fabric adhesive
Bodkin
Matching thread

FOR THE LAMPSHADE

Net fabric – see below for
  quantity
Chenille braid
2cm (¾in) diameter polystyrene

balls
Fabric adhesive
Matching thread

FOR THE CLOTH

Net fabric – see below for
  quantity
Chenille braid

Feathers
Fabric adhesive
Matching thread

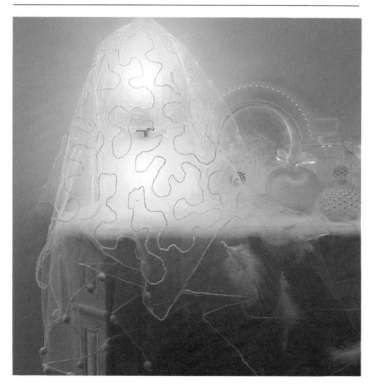

METHOD

THE DOOR CURTAIN

▦ Measure the door and cut a length of net fabric to this size, plus 2cm (1in) on the width and 7cm (3in) on the length, for top casing and hems.

▦ Turn under a double 6mm (¼in) wide hem on side and base edges of curtain, making neat base corners. Pin, tack and stitch hems in place.

▦ At the top edge, turn under a double 3cm (1¼in) wide hem to form a casing; pin, tack and stitch in place along the lower folded edge.

▦ Using fabric adhesive, fix braid haphazardly over the curtain in a loopy design, adding polystyrene balls. Push a hole straight through the centre of each ball with a bodkin and push in the folded braid, till the end just comes through on the opposite side.

▦ Add appliqué shapes: decide on a simple flower and leaf design and mark the shapes onto the fabric. Stitch round each shape just inside the outline. Cut out each shape. Pin appliqué shapes onto the curtain, set your sewing-machine to a close zigzag stitch and work round each shape. Add trails of braid for stamens.

▦ Thread on covered wire and hang above the door.

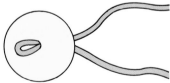

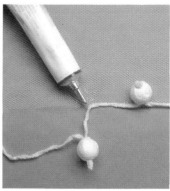

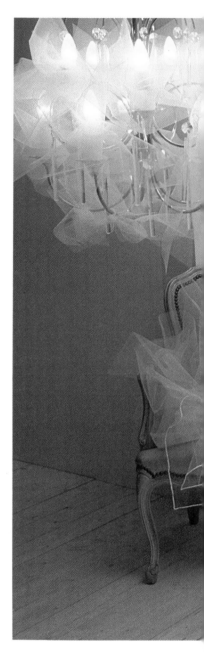

THE LAMPSHADE

▦ Measure from the centre of the top of the existing lampshade to the desired length of the cover and cut out a square to twice this length.

▦ Turn up a tiny hem to the right side and handstitch in place with small stitches. Stick braid over the raw edge, with edge butting against the outer edge of the cover, adding polystyrene balls at intervals, as for the door curtain.

▦ Cut a 5cm (2in) diameter hole

from the centre of the square. Neaten and finish the edge with braid in the same way as the hem edge.

▦ Add haphazard patterns of braid all over the square.

▦ Place the net cover over the existing lampshade. Make sure that your lampshade will keep the net at a safe distance from the light bulb, so that there is no danger that it might catch fire, and use a low wattage bulb. Never try to cover a live flame,

even if the distance between the flame and the net seems safe.

THE CLOTH

▦ Cut a square of fabric to the desired size and finish the outer edge as for the lampshade.

▦ Work tiny bars in the cloth at positions chosen for the feathers. Slot the feathers through the bars to hold them in place (in this way they can easily be removed when you need to wash the cloth).

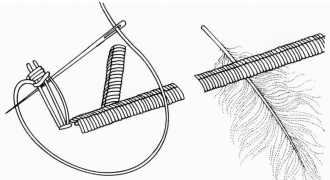

DAMASK DELIGHT

Sprays of pink and creamy flowers and grasses – unashamedly feminine and romantic – are set against a slightly unusual background of chequered pink damask, creating a feeling of elegance and great charm. The resulting tablecloth would look equally at home in a formal dining room, perhaps complemented by bowls of fresh flowers, or spread over a garden table. A matching cloth of striped pink-and-white cotton underneath protects the carefully embroidered damask and could be used to give it greater coverage.

Size 194cm × 194cm (77½in × 77½in).

MATERIALS

200cm × 200cm (80in × 80in) of pink-and-white chequered damask fabric Matching thread	Dressmakers' carbon paper Crewel needle size 4 or 5 Large embroidery hoop

Threads

DMC stranded cotton: one skein each of **grey** 415 and 452, **green** 368 and 3051, **pink** 335, 776, 778 and 819, and **blue grey** 927; two skeins each of **grey** 3024, **green** 3053, **pink** 223 and 3354, and **dull gold** 3032, and three skeins each of **green** 369, **grey** 642, and **beige** 822

Embroidery stitches

Long and short stitch, straight stitch, satin stitch, stem stitch and seed stitch.

METHOD

THE EMBROIDERY

▦ Trace the flower design and enlarge it to the required dimensions as shown on page 10. This is a complex design, and you may find that it helps if you number each square on both the smaller and larger grids when you are enlarging the pattern. Alternatively, you may prefer to concentrate on copying the main outlines accurately, filling in the smaller details by hand: your design may vary from the original, but only in minor respects.

▦ Using the photograph as a guide, transfer the motif to the corner of the fabric, using the carbon paper method given on page 11 and position the design approximately 45cm (18in) in from the raw edges of the fabric.

▦ Working with the fabric stretched in the embroidery hoop, embroider the large flowers and areas of foliage in long and short stitch and the clusters of smaller flowers in satin stitch. Work the stems in stem stitch and the grasses in seed stitch and straight stitch.

▦ Use the photograph and the design as a guide when blending the colours, and work with four strands of thread for solid colour areas and for shaded areas.

▦ When the embroidery is finished, place the fabric face down on a well-padded surface and press it lightly, taking care not to crush the stitches.

FINISHING

▦ Following a line of the chequer pattern, turn a double 2cm (¾in) hem to the wrong side all around. Either make straight folds at the corners, or cut away spare fabric diagonally and make mitred folds.

▦ Pin and stitch the hem in place.

N/O A/N

B, E, C, D

KEY

To enlarge the design, first draw a grid on tracing paper, each square measuring 5mm × 5mm (¼in × ¼in). Trace over the main outlines of the design, then enlarge it onto a 2.5cm (1in) grid. Fill in any details by hand and transfer the design to the fabric. The letters show which colours are used in particular areas: where two letters are given together, for example H/K, use two strands of each colour in the needle.

A 927	M 819
B 642	N 415
C 3024	O 452
D 822	P 3051
E 369	R 3053
F 368	S 3032
G 776	
H 223	
J 335	
K 3354	
L 778	

B/E/C/D

P/E

E

A/N, N/O

B/F

A/N, N/O

B/F

D, E, K
G/M, K/M

S/H, G/M, D, G, M

F/
R

E

K, G, M, L

E, F,
P/R

B/F

E, F,
P/R, F/P

B/F

K, M, G, H,

K, G, H, D, K/M

L/D, S/H

B/E/C/D

E
F

F/R
B/F

E

F

F/E

K, G

E

F, E,
P/R, F/P

M, G, K, M/G,
S/H/M

P/E

F/E

E

P/E

F/R

P/R, F/P, R/E

E
F/R

R/E

K, G, H, D
K/G

B/F

F, E, P/R
F/P

F/R

L, G, M, K/M, G/M, K/G, H/J

K G H
H/J

F

E

F, E, P/R, F/P

K G H D
H/J

E

L

R/E

B/F

F/R
R/E

F

F

E F E

B/E, C, D

B, E, C, D

R/E

F

E

B/F

E

B/F

E
F/R

K, G, H, H/K

F

A/N, N, O

B/F

☆ C, A, L, D, M, D/K

☆ M/K, G/K, D/K, M, D, L, J

N/O

SEASHELL TRACERY

The delicate traces of seashells are worked in white satin stitch on a padded panel of navy cotton chintz. The embroidered square is then bordered with navy-and-white-striped cotton and 'framed' with the navy chintz – the entire panel is attached to a plain white cotton sheet to create a stylish bed throw.

MATERIALS

1.5m (1½yd) × 115cm (45in) wide navy blue cotton chintz
60cm (2ft) × 60cm (2ft) polyester wadding
60cm (2ft) × 60cm (2ft) fine calico
70cm (28in) × 90cm (36in) wide navy-and-white-striped cotton

White dressmaker's pencil
Knitting needle
White sewing thread
Chenille needle size 18 or 20
Navy sewing thread
White cotton sheet, single-bed size

Thread
50gm (2 oz) ball of white knitting cotton, 4-ply weight

Embroidery Stitch
Satin stitch

METHOD

▦ From the navy chintz cut out one square 62cm (24½in) × 62cm (24½in) and four strips each 19cm (7½in) × 103cm (41in).

▦ From the striped cotton cut four strips 5.5cm (2¼in) × 64cm (25½in) wide, across the stripes.

▦ Enlarge the design to the dimensions given on the pattern.

▦ Pierce each small dot on the full-size pattern with the point of the knitting needle, then place the pattern over the chintz square and mark the dots on the right side of the fabric with the dressmaker's pencil.

▦ Place wadding between the chintz and the calico, making sure the chintz is right side up. There should be 1cm (⅜in) surplus of chintz all round the square. Pin through the three layers to hold them in place before tacking together vertically and horizontally, using the white sewing thread.

▦ Embroider the dots in satin stitch with the knitting cotton. Then work the remaining motifs in the same way, using the diagram as a guide to the placement.

▦ Remove the tacking threads and press the 1cm (⅜in) surplus of chintz to the wrong side, taking care not to flatten the wadding.

▦ To make the narrow striped border, machine stitch the striped sections together at the corners as shown in the diagram using the navy thread.

▦ To make the wide chintz 'frame' machine stitch the chintz strips at the four angles shown in the diagram.

▦ Place the striped border

centrally on the white sheet and pin it in position. Then put the embroidered chintz square in the centre of the striped border and tack in position. Machine stitch around the edge of the square, keeping the stitches as close to the edge as possible. Remove the tacking thread.

▦ Turn and press a 1 cm (⅜in) hem on the inner and outer edges of the chintz 'frame' and position it around the edge of the striped border, overlapping it by 1 cm (⅜in) to hide the raw edges. Pin and then tack it in place. Machine stitch around the inner and outer edges of the 'frame', as close to the edge as possible. Remove the tacking stitches.

▦ Press the chintz frame and border carefully, but do not press the embroidered chintz square or the wadding will be flattened.

Taking inspiration from nature, the stylized forms of the shells above have been reproduced on the bed throw. By simplifying other natural forms, an endless variety of fascinating designs can be created.

The shell shapes are worked in dots and blocks of satin stitch on the central padded section. This is framed firstly by a narrow striped border and then by a wide, plain navy blue border.

169

VARIATIONS IN GREEN

In some hot countries, the people weave leafy branches above their beds to create a cool atmosphere: this tender green design could have the same soothing effect. It features fronds of the castor-oil plant, copied from a botanical drawing and worked in a wide range of greens to create a realistic effect. The design here is shown on a large pillow of a type not generally found outside France, so the quantities and dimensions quoted have been adjusted to make a standard single duvet cover.

Size 136cm × 200cm (54in × 80in).

MATERIALS

6.3m (7yd) of 140cm (56in) wide white fabric with an even weave	Dressmakers' carbon paper in a dark colour
1m (1yd) of nylon press stud tape	Crewel needle size 3 or 4
White sewing thread	Large embroidery hoop

Threads

DMC pearl cotton No. 5: two skeins each of **grey** 644, 647 and 648; **green** 320, 367, 368, 369, 469, 470, 471, 472, 500, 503, 504, 703, 904, 911, 954, 966, 987 and 989, and (optional) two skeins of DMC stranded cotton in **white** (if you wish to make a drawn-threadwork hem)

Embroidery stitches

Straight stitch, running stitch, stem stitch, Chinese knots, back stitch and hem stitch (optional).

METHOD

The designer used an old cover with a drawn-threadwork pattern and superimposed her own design over this. The drawn-threadwork hem stitching is not an essential part of the design, and it would be simpler to omit the lines running straight across the leaf design. If you decide to keep the lines of drawn-threadwork which border the design and edge the frill, make these before beginning the leaf embroidery.

Cut the two main pieces, each measuring 140cm × 209.5cm (56in × 83¾in) from the fabric. Cut the remaining fabric into 20cm (8in) wide strips and join these to make a continuous strip for the frill. Turn under and press a double 1cm (⅜in) hem along one edge. If you are not working a decorative edge, stitch the hem of the frill in the ordinary way.

If you are working the hem-stitched borders, make them at this stage along the hem of the frill and running parallel to the sides of the main fabric piece, 15cm (6in) in from the raw edges, using the photograph as a guide to position. Stitch the borders in the same way as the border of the napkin on page 108, catching in the hem along the frill and making a purely decorative border (no hem) around the main fabric piece.

Trace the leaf design and enlarge it to the required dimensions, following the instructions given on page 10. Using dressmakers' carbon paper, transfer the design to the centre of the fabric.

Working with the fabric stretched in the embroidery hoop and using the photograph as a colour and stitch guide, embroider the leaf design mainly in straight stitch and running stitch,

strengthening the outlines with back stitch and stem stitch. Use Chinese knots to pick out the details on the seeds.

▦ When the embroidery is finished, place the fabric face down on a well-padded surface and press it lightly, taking care not to crush the stitches.

FINISHING THE COVER
▦ Divide the frill into four equal

sections and mark with pins. Gather each frill section in turn.

▦ Mark the central point on the *seamline* at each edge of the front section of the cover. The seamline is 7.5cm (3in) in from the raw edge along the bottom and 2cm (¾in) in along the remaining three sides.

▦ Position the frill on the front, with right sides matching and the finished edge of the frill lying

inwards. The frill has a 1.5cm seam allowance, so match seamlines, not raw edges.

▦ Matching marked points, pull up the gathering stitches of each section of the frill in turn. Pin and stitch the frill in place along the edges of the front.

▦ Trim the seam allowance on the frill only to 6mm (¼in). Finish the cover as described for the cover on page 152.

KEY

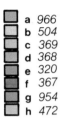	a	966		i	989		q	503
	b	504		j	904		r	500
	c	369		k	471		s	648
	d	368		l	470		t	644
	e	320		m	469		u	647
	f	367		n	911			
	g	954		o	987			
	h	472		p	703			

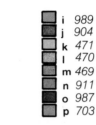

SPRINGTIME DREAM

This lavishly embroidered, luxuriously feminine bedcover, with its matching pillowcases, was inspired by four new varieties of tulip: Greenland, pink and tender green; Angélique, luscious as a peony; Shirley, ivory tinged with purple, and Dreaming Mead, with its lovely closed buds. You can either embroider the designs by hand, as seen in the picture, carefully blending the different shades like a skilled artist, or for quicker results you could machine embroider the flowers and leaves, using variegated threads. An even speedier method would be to paint the design, using fabric paints and taking care to make delicately shaded petals. The flowers, stems and leaves might be outlined in stem stitch and selected areas highlighted with satin stitching.

Size: bedcover 230cm × 220cm (92in × 87in); pillowcases 90cm × 62cm (36in × 24¾in), including scalloped edges.

MATERIALS

3.8m (4¼yd) of 228cm (90in) wide fine cotton or linen fabric
DMC stranded cotton as follows: two skeins each of green 92, 369 and 703, and ecru; one skein each of green 94, 471, 472, 580, 966, 987, 989 and 3347, white, pink 62, 106, 112, 602, 603, 604, 760, 761, 776, 819, 892, 893, 948, 3326 and 3689, blue 828 and yellow 445
or machine embroidery cottons in variegated pinks and greens
or fabric paints and a range of paint brushes with green and pink stranded cottons for outlining the designs
2 reels of DMC machine embroidery cotton in pale pink No. 50, for scalloped edges of pillowcases
Pink coloured pencil
Crewel needle size 7 or 8
Tracing paper
Dressmakers' carbon paper
Large embroidery hoop
Matching thread
Note If the above yarn is unobtainable, refer to page 191.

174

METHOD

▦ Cut one piece of fabric 246cm (98in) long, cutting across the full width, for the bedcover. For the pillowcases, cut two pieces 90cm × 62cm (36in × 24¾in) for the tops and two pieces 90cm × 50cm (36in × 20in) for the underneath.

▦ On the bedcover piece, make 2cm (¾in) double hems down the sides, and 4cm (1½in) double hems at the top and bottom.

▦ Starting from the corners measure out evenly spaced scallops around the edges of the pillowcase tops and draw them on the fabric in coloured pencil. Embroider the scallops in pink machine embroidery cotton,

using machine satin stitch 4mm (³⁄₁₆in) wide.

▦ Enlarge the design for the bedcover onto tracing paper and transfer it to the cover with dressmakers' carbon paper (see page 11), using the photograph as a guide to position.

▦ Transfer the pillowcase design to the pillowcase tops in the same manner.

▦ Embroider the tulip motifs in long and short stitch, using the charts as colour guides and the photograph as a stitch guide. Two strands of thread are used throughout and the stitches should be between 3mm (⅛in) and 4mm (³⁄₁₆in) long to achieve the painted effect shown on the photograph. Work with the fabric

stretched in an embroidery hoop, moving it as necessary.

▦ If you wish to work the design in machine embroidery, first stitch the main outlines by hand in stem stitch. Then put the fabric in a small embroidery hoop: lay the fabric right side up over the outer ring, then place the inner ring over it, so the fabric can lie flat on the base plate of your machine. Set the machine to straight running stitch and lower the feeding teeth so that you can move the ring around freely until each area is filled with stitching. The speed with which you move the ring about will govern the length of the stitches, so work a practice piece first.

▦ When the embroidery is

complete, place it face downwards on a well-padded surface and press it lightly, taking care not to crush the stitches.

▦ To complete the pillowcases, for each pillowcase take an underneath section and make 1cm (³⁄₈in) double hems down all four sides. Bring over a 12cm (4¾in) deep fold of fabric to the wrong side across one short end and tack at the sides.

▦ With wrong sides together, centre underneath section over pillowcase top, taking care that scalloped edges extend evenly all around. Pin and tack together, then topstitch or stabstitch along the two long sides and the unfolded short end. Remove tacking and insert pillow.

175

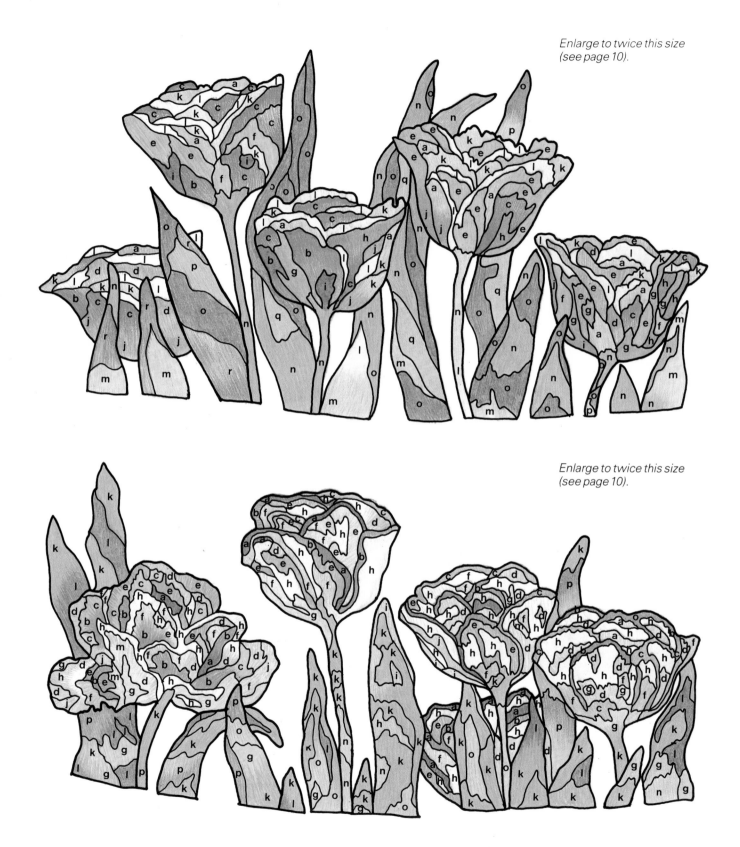

*Enlarge to twice this size
(see page 10).*

*Enlarge to twice this size
(see page 10).*

Enlarge to twice this size
(see page 10).

KEY

Top left					
a 948	**n** 989	**h** white	**d** 3347		
b 112	**o** 987	**i** 828	**e** 369		
c 106	**p** 472	**j** 948	**f** 819		
d 62	**q** 966	**k** 989	**g** 776		
e 776	**r** 92	**l** 987	**h** 471		
f 761		**m** 445	**i** 3689		
g 760	Bottom left	**n** 472	**j** 948		
h 893	**a** 602	**o** 966	**k** 760		
i 892	**b** 603	**p** 92	**l** 761		
j 3326	**c** 604		**m** 604		
k 819	**d** 819	Above	**n** 471	**r** 603	
l white	**e** 776	**a** ecru	**o** 94	**s** 472	
m 369	**f** ecru	**b** white	**p** 703	**t** 966	
	g 369	**c** 3326	**q** 92	**u** 580	

177

CEREMONIAL CHIC

Create a family heirloom by working on the best of materials: a beautiful damask tablecloth, woven with a geometric design. Each square is filled with finely worked circles, triangles and bars in shiny pastels, with zigzags and bars and bows and knots. You could adapt the idea too – wavy lines or circles worked round the damask motifs of any beautiful old linen cloth will be just as original. Or embroider a beautiful length of fabric to make a party skirt or dance frock.

MATERIALS

White and silver cotton damask fabric, to make a cloth. (Alternatively, the silver lines can be added to white fabric by machining zigzag lines across the length and width of the fabric, using a fine metallic machine thread.)
Crewel needle size 6 or 7
Crewel needle size 4
HB pencil
Embroidery hoop

Threads
Anchor stranded cotton in the following colours:
blue 128, 130; **green** 187, 238, 253; **kingfisher blue** 433; **turquoise** 185; **pale tan** 347; **yellow** 292, 297; **pink** 48, 54, 968; **grey** 397; **cream** 386; **beige** 830
DMC **fil d'argent** 280

Embroidery Stitches
Satin stitch, straight stitch, cross stitch, knots (see diagram).

METHOD

▣ Use the photographs as a guide to the placement of the motifs and for the colours. Draw the circles, squares and triangles lightly on the fabric with the HB pencil.

▣ Work with the fabric stretched in an embroidery hoop, moving the hoop as each section is completed.

▣ Embroider the circles, squares and triangles in satin stitch using three strands of thread and the finer crewel needle; take care to cover the pencil lines completely.

▣ Work the zigzags and bars at random (without pencil guidelines which would be difficult to conceal) in straight stitch, using either three strands of cotton or one strand of silver thread.

▣ Next, add the cross stitch and the 'V' shapes in straight stitch, again using three strands of cotton or one of silver.

▣ Place the cloth face down on a well-padded surface and press lightly, taking care not to crush the stitches.

▣ Then add the 'bows' by making simple knots, as shown in the diagram, with either six strands of cotton or two strands of silver thread.

▣ To make up the cloth, turn a double hem all round (see page 14 for instructions on mitring corners) and either machine or hand stitch.

The 'bows' – knotted and cut threads.

178

traditional wedding cloth with a modern gloss

Multi-sized circles in a haphazard arrangement are satin-stitched in a variety of hues.

Mix squares, circles and triangles, completing the design with zigzags of colour.

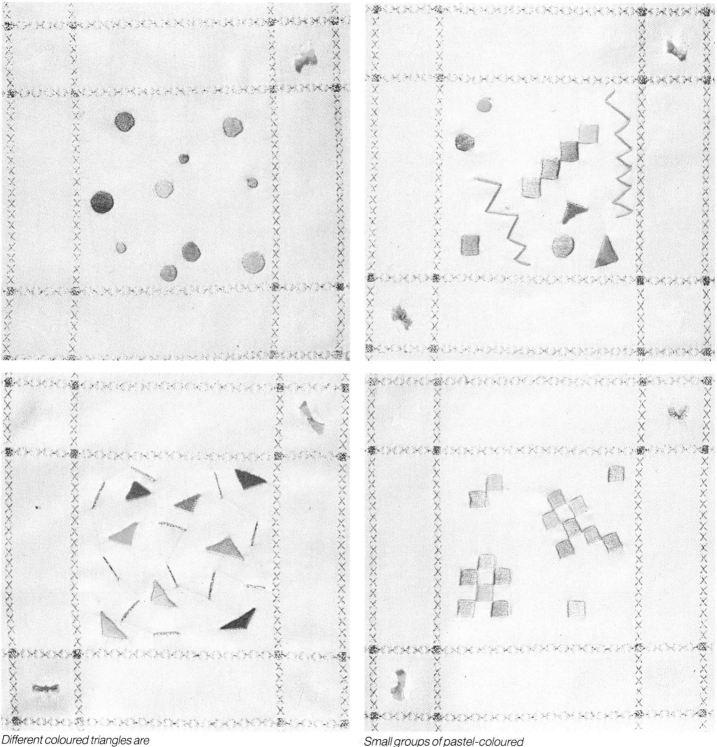

Different coloured triangles are interspersed with bars of silver, which match the cross-stitching.

Small groups of pastel-coloured squares, straight or slanted make for a pleasing arrangement.

180

Just triangles in bright colours all the same size. Match up with thread bows at the corners.

Pick three colours and make up thread bows to fill the square. Add silver cross stitches.

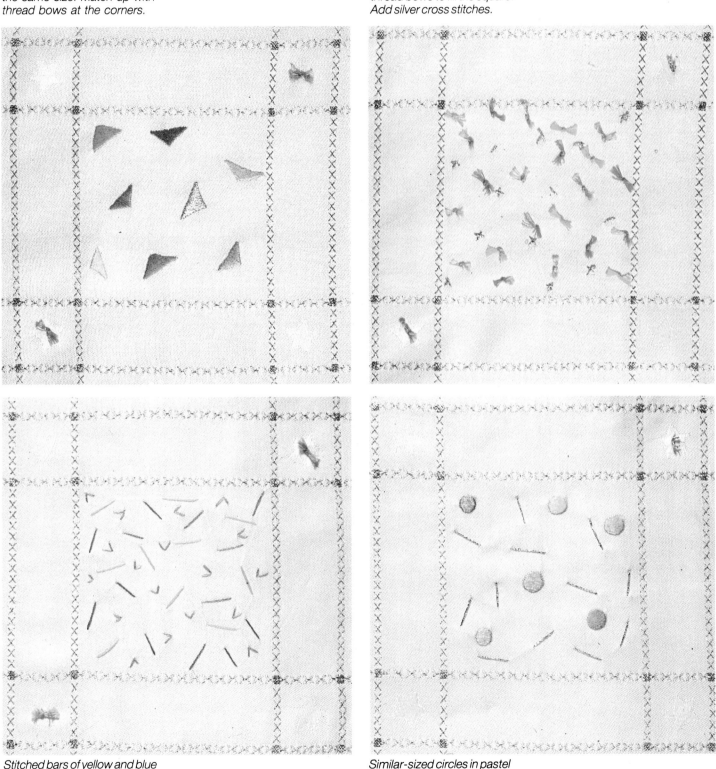

Stitched bars of yellow and blue mingle with green V-shapes. Complete with thread bows.

Similar-sized circles in pastel shades are split up by bars of silver.

GEOMETRIC PERFECTION

Dark blue embroidery on pure white cotton piqué makes an elegant and unusual floor covering, visually interesting yet at the same time in perfect harmony with the cool, uncluttered modern style. White cotton might seem impractical as a floor covering – and indeed you could equally well use this as a wall hanging or a bed throw – but it is machine washable. If you have time to spare, you could even embroider a kimono to match.

Size: 130cm × 130cm (52in × 52in).

MATERIALS

2.7m (3yd) of 135cm (54in) wide
   white cotton piqué
2.7m (3yd) of 90cm (36in) wide
   lightweight polyester wadding
DMC coton à broder: 35 skeins of

blue 2336
Tracing paper
Dressmakers' carbon paper
Matching thread

METHOD

▦ Cut two pieces of cotton piqué, each measuring 133cm × 133cm (53½in × 53½in). Also cut two lengths of wadding, each 130cm long.

▦ Place the strips of wadding side by side and herringbone stitch the edges together. Turn the pieces the other way up and repeat the process. Trim the resulting piece of wadding to measure 130cm × 130cm (52in × 52in).

▦ Draw a grid on tracing paper and scale up the design. Position the tracing paper over the centre of one fabric square, on the right side of the fabric, and pin both fabric and paper to a flat surface, pinning around the edge of the design. Slide the carbon paper, right side down, between the fabric and the paper design. Because of the scale of the design, you may find it necessary to work section by section. Trace over the design, marking it on the fabric.

▦ Leaving an even 1.5cm (⅝in) margin of cotton piqué all around, pin and tack the polyester wadding to the wrong side of the marked cotton. Place the wadded and unwadded cotton squares with right sides together and pin, tack and stitch together

around the outer edge, taking a 1.5cm (⅝in) seam allowance and leaving a gap for turning.

▦ Turn the square right side out, enclosing the wadding. Fold in seam allowances along the gap and slipstitch to close.

▦ Smooth out the three layers and make lines of tacking across the fabric, vertically and horizontally, at intervals of about 10cm (4in), taking care not to ruckle the layers.

▦ Using three strands of embroidery cotton in your needle, embroider the design. The dots marked A consist of a cluster of seven French knots, as shown on page 184. The section of the design marked B is worked in a graduated satin stitch. It is not essential that all stitches should pass through all three layers, but the layers should be held together at intervals of approximately 10cm (4in), or the finished mat may tend to ruckle.

▦ When the central design is complete, topstitch all around the mat in matching thread, 2cm (¾in) from the outer edge.

▦ Using three strands of embroidery cotton, complete the design with diagonal lines of large darning stitches across the undecorated section, stitching through all layers and finishing off neatly.

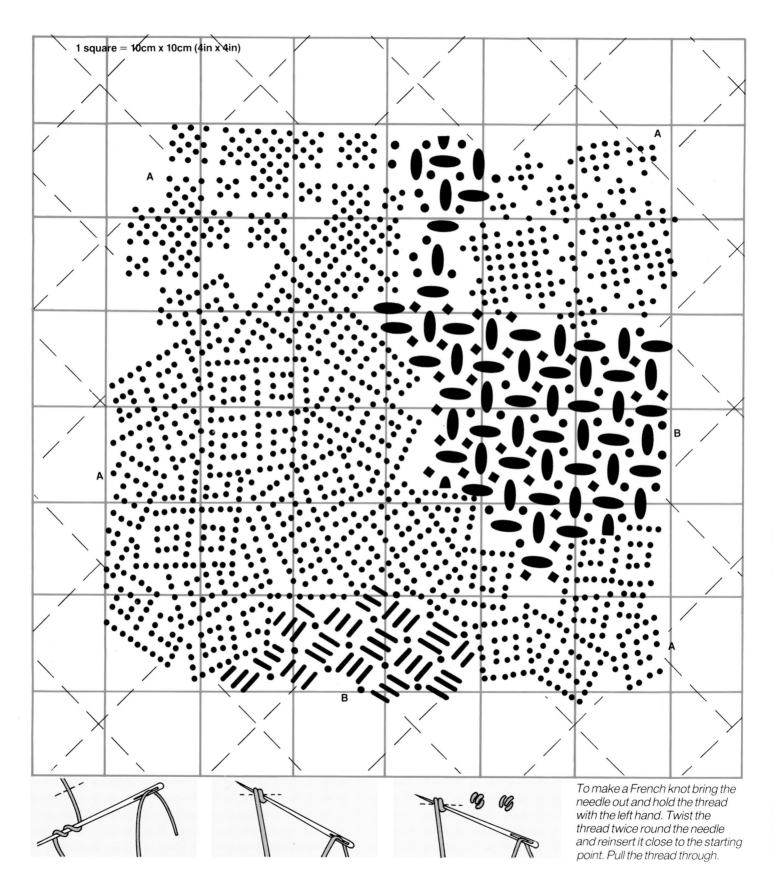

1 square = 10cm x 10cm (4in x 4in)

To make a French knot bring the needle out and hold the thread with the left hand. Twist the thread twice round the needle and reinsert it close to the starting point. Pull the thread through.

The pattern shown opposite can equally be applied to a shirt (or kimono) as to a rug. The colour scheme has been reversed (above), to striking effect.

CHINA BLUE, POPPY RED

Blue-and-white porcelain vases are filled with the glorious tulips and poppies of late spring and early summer. No-one would pretend that these luxurious cushion covers are the sort of thing that you can complete in a day, but there is a great deal of pleasure to be gained from working with such a rich, lustrous and varied range of colours, and even more satisfaction to come, when your friends compliment you on the finished cushions.

Size Approximately 60cm × 60cm (24in × 24in).

MATERIALS

FOR ONE COVER
1.4m (1½yd) of 90cm (36in) wide closely woven white cotton fabric
Matching sewing thread
Crewel needle size 6 or 7

Large embroidery hoop
Tracing paper
Dressmakers' carbon paper
40cm (16in) zip

Threads
FOR THE TULIP CUSHION
DMC stranded cotton: one skein each of **pink** 353, 604, 605, 776, 778, 818, 962, 3326 and 3684, **yellow** 742, 743, 744, 972 and 973, **flesh** 948, **orange** 741, **peach** 754, **apricot** 352, **white, ecru, grey beige** 644, **wine** 814, **green** 320, 368, 703, 987, 988 and 989, **mauve** 316, and **blue** 800, and three skeins of **blue** 798

FOR THE POPPY CUSHION
DMC stranded cotton: one skein each of **wine** 814, 3685 and 902, **orange** 741 and 947, **apricot** 350 and 351, **blue** 800, **yellow** 725 and 742, **black** 310, **green** 703, 704, 904, 906, 907, 988 and 989, **rust** 817, and **pink** 353; two skeins each of **red** 321 and 498, **orange** 608, and **apricot** 352; three skeins of **blue** 798, and four skeins each of **red** 606 and 666.

Embroidery stitches
TULIP CUSHION
Long and short stitch, satin stitch, stem stitch and chain stitch.

POPPY CUSHION
Long and short stitch, satin stitch, stem stitch and Chinese knots.

METHOD

TULIP CUSHION
▨ Cut a 70cm × 70cm (28in × 28in) square of cotton fabric. Cut two more pieces, each 63cm × 33cm (25¼in × 13¼in) and set these to one side.
▨ Scale up the design onto tracing paper and transfer it to the centre of the fabric square, using dressmakers' carbon paper (see page 11).

▨ Work with the fabric stretched in an embroidery hoop, moving it as necessary. Three strands of thread are used throughout.
▨ Embroider the tulips and leaves in long and short stitch and the stems in satin stitch, using the chart as a colour guide. No two people would reproduce this design exactly the same, stitch for stitch; the important thing is to embroider each petal separately, making sure that the colour

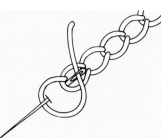

chain stitch

changes blend gradually into each other, to give the effect of the subtle variations of tone to be found on flower petals.
▨ Work the vase mainly in satin stitch, picking out the details in stem stitch and the arabesques in chain stitch, using the photograph as a stitch guide.
▨ When the embroidery is complete, place it face down on a well-padded surface and press it lightly, taking care not to crush the stitches. Trim to measure 63cm (25¼in) square.
▨ Take the other two pieces of cotton fabric and place them right sides together. Pin and tack together down one long side, taking a 1.5cm (⅝in) seam allowance. At either side, stitch from the raw edge towards the centre for 11.5cm (4⅝in), leaving a gap for the zip. Insert zip.
▨ With right sides together and zip open, pin, tack and stitch cushion back to cushion front, stitching all around the outside and taking a 1.5cm (⅝in) seam allowance. Turn right side out.

POPPY CUSHION
▨ Cut fabric, scale up and transfer design as for tulip cushion. Work with the fabric in an embroidery hoop, using three strands of cotton throughout.
▨ Embroider the flowers in long and short stitch and the stems in satin stitch, using the chart as a colour guide. Pick out the poppy seeds in Chinese knots, using black thread. Work the vase mainly in satin stitch, with stem stitch for the linear details, using the photograph as a stitch guide.
▨ Press the finished embroidery and make up the cushion cover as for the tulip cushion.

KEY FOR TULIP CUSHION

a	*353*	**q**	*352*
b	*604*	**r**	*white*
c	*605*	**s**	*ecru*
d	*776*	**t**	*644*
e	*778*	**u**	*814*
f	*818*	**v**	*320*
g	*3326*	**w**	*368*
h	*368*	**x**	*987*
i	*742*	**y**	*988*
j	*743*	**z**	*989*
k	*744*	**A**	*316*
l	*972*	**B**	*800*
m	*973*	**C**	*798*
n	*948*	**D**	*445*
o	*741*	**E**	*307*
p	*754*	**F**	*602*

KEY FOR POPPY CUSHION

a	*814*	**n**	*906*
b	*3685*	**o**	*817*
c	*741*	**p**	*321*
d	*947*	**q**	*608*
e	*350*	**r**	*352*
f	*351*	**s**	*353*
g	*800*	**t**	*798*
h	*725*	**u**	*606*
i	*742*	**v**	*666*
j	*310*	**w**	*743*
k	*703*	**x**	*922*
l	*704*		
m	*904*		

THREAD AND YARN OPTIONS

Some of the embroidery threads and rug yarns listed in this book may be difficult to obtain outside France. If you have problems in finding the listed yarns, the alternatives given below can be used as perfectly acceptable substitutes. In all cases, the French thread or yarn shade number is quoted first, followed by the shade number of the substitute, and the number of skeins or hanks of each substitute shade should be as specified for the original.

IKEBANA
For DMC rug yarn, substitute Patons Turkey rug wool in cut packs as follows: DMC 7143/Patons 958; 7520/939; black/903; 7107/850; 7120/877; 7384/960; 7850/838; 7504/919; ecru/50; 7305/922; 7505/858 and 7202/943

SCATTERED FLOWERS
For DMC tapestry yarn, substitute Anchor tapestry yarn as follows: white rose DMC 7321/Anchor 3363; 7333/0505; white/white; 7431/0288; 7745/0305; 7320/0654 and 7384/0215
pink rose – 7431/0288; 7786/3421; 7200/0892; 7202/024; 7204/0895; 7445/3186; 7362/0647; 7382/0242; 7542/0579 and white/white
yellow rose – 7445/3186; 7579/0729; 7726/0295; 7727/0306; white/white; 7369/0859; 7370/3150; 7548/3234 and 7584/0279

COLOUR AND LIGHT
For DMC rug yarn, substitute uncut hanks of Readicut rug yarn as follows: DMC 7333/Readicut 50; ecru/38; 7504/21; 7313/12; black/48; 7505/88; 7301/35; 7305/23; 7307/37; 7317/74; 7326/45; 7120/72; 7196/51; 7202/86; 7206/94; 7491/40; 7347/22; 7520/87; 7421/44; 7446/3 and 7444/1

BUTTERFLY PICNIC
For DMC stranded cotton, substitute Anchor stranded cotton as follows: DMC 300/Anchor 0352; 976/0309; 310/0403; 413/0400; 444/0291; 676/0891; 742/0303; 972/0298; 973/0290; 792/0941; 799/0130; 800/0128; 995/0410; 996/0433; 553/098; 701/0229; 907/0255; 943/0188; 991/0212; and 993/0186

SPRINGTIME DREAM
For DMC stranded cotton, substitute Anchor stranded cotton as follows: DMC 92/Anchor 1215; 369/0213; 703/0239; ecru/0926; 94/1216; 471/0265; 472/0253; 580/0268; 966/0206; 987/0258; 989/0256; 3347/0266; white/02; 62/1201; 106/1203; 112/1204; 602/077; 603/076; 604/075; 760/09; 761/08; 776/025; 819/023; 892/028; 893/027; 948/0933; 3326/026; 3689/073; 828/0158 and 445/0288

ACKNOWLEDGMENTS

2	Burgi/Lebeau
5	Duffas/Garcon
6	Godeaut/Faver
7 top left	Dirand/Lebeau
7 top right	Bouchet/Lebeau
7 below	Tisne/Garcon
8-9	Dirand/Lebeau
11	Laiter/Garcon
12	Bouchet/Chabaneix
13 top left	Bouchet/Lebeau
13 top right	Duffas/Garcon
16-17	Dirand/Lebeau
18-20	M Duffas/J Schoumacher
23-26	B Maltaverne/C Lebeau
27-28	M Duffas/I Garcon
30-33	M Duffas/I Garcon
34-35	J Dirand/C Lebeau
39	M Duffas/I Garcon
42-44	M Duffas/I Garcon
46-47	A Bianchi/I Garcon
49	G De Chabaneix/A Lurtz
52	N Bruant/C Lebeau
53	C Lebeau/Lebeau
56-57	B Maltaverne/Marion Faver
60-61	B Maltaverne/C Lebeau
64-65	Tisne/Garcon
66-67	E Novick/I Garcon
69	M Duffas/I Garcon
70-71	M Duronsoy/A Jacobs
72-73	J Tisne/I Garcon
76-77	J Tisne/I Garcon
78-79	J P Godeaut/M Faver
80-81	A Bianchi/I Garcon

84-85	B Maltaverne/C Lebeau
86-87	Bouchet/Lebeau
88-89	M Duffas/I Garcon
91	G Bouchet/C Lebeau
92-95	M Duffas/J Schoumacher
96-99	M Duffas/J Schoumacher
100-101	G. de Chabaneix/C Lebeau
102-105	G Bouchet/C de Chabaneix
106-107	M Duffas/J Schoumacher
109	J Dirand/C Lebeau
110-111	M Duffas/I Garcon
114-115	B Maltaverne/C Lebeau
116-121	M Duffas/I Garcon
122-123	M Duffas/J Schoumacher
124-129	J Dirand/C Lebeau
130-133	V Assenat/J Schoumacher
134-137	B Maltaverne/C Lebeau
138-141	D de Chabaneix/I Garcon
143-145	Duffas/Schoumacher/Garcon
146-147	Duffas/Garcon
150-151	Duffas/Schoumacher
152-156	Chabaneix/Garcon
158-160	Chabaneix/Chabaneix
162-163	Duffas/Schoumacher
164-166	Assenat/Schoumacher
168-169	Bruant/Lebeau
170-172	Bouchet/Lebeau
174-175	Chabaneix/Garcon
180-181	Bianchi/Garcon
182-183	Burgi/Lebeau
184-185	Burgi/Lebeau
186-188	Dirand/Lebeau